DREAM CARS

DREAM CARS

Andrew Frankel

Abbeville Press Publishers
New York London

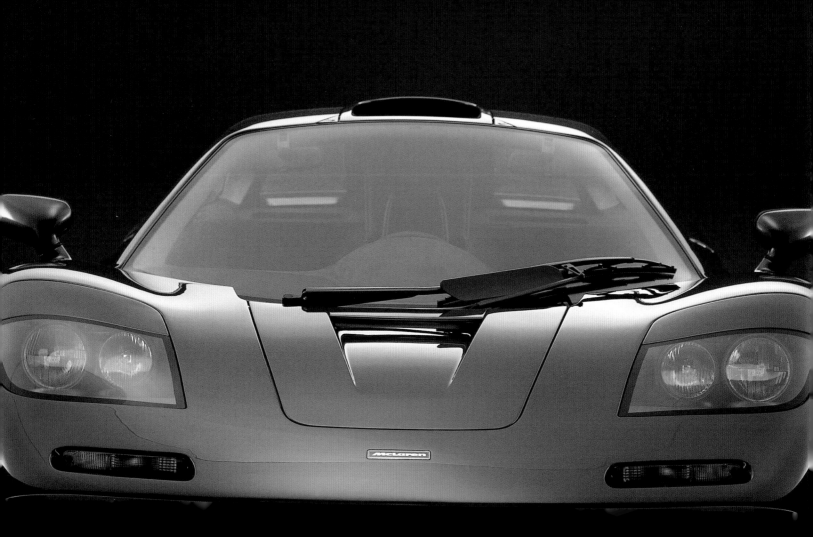

CONTENTS

PREFACE TO THE 2ND EDITION

It doesn't seem nearly ten years since I first sat down to write *Dream Cars*, but looking at the cars I chose to include in my top fifty supercars, I cannot help noticing that machines which then represented the absolute state-of-the-art, such as the Ferrari F50, are now regarded as classics.

We have come such a long way in the intervening years: cars like the Porsche Carrera GT, Ferrari Enzo, Mercedes-Benz McLaren SLR, Maserati MC12 and Aston Martin DB9 have rewritten the supercar rule book and raised the level of road car performance onto a plane beyond almost any in this book. I say "almost'" because what I find most interesting is that, despite the technological gains of the last decade, the performance of the McLaren F1 —itself not a new car when the first *Dream Cars* was published—has still yet to be matched, let alone eclipsed. At the time it was the fastest road car there had ever been and so it remains today.

I have sought to update *Dream Cars* for new readers, quoting new production numbers for cars that were still being built when the book first appeared and recording the date when, finally, they left the stage. Some of the cars have evolved considerably in the intervening years and, for instance, the Lotus Elise of today is a very different animal from that which first appeared on these pages. In all cases, the text and technical specifications refer specifically to the cars in the photographs, and not to any later iterations.

I have, however, allowed myself the liberty of including one new car, Ford's extraordinary new GT. It's neither the fastest nor the most expensive car in this book, but for its extraordinary appearance and phenomenal appetite for the open road, I felt it had earned its place between these covers. I hope you enjoy reading about it and the fifty other classic machines featured here as much as I did driving and writing about them.

INTRODUCTION

There is no definition of what does, or does not, add up to a dream car. It's not that they go quickly; some of the most unpleasant cars I have ever driven have covered the ground at a terrifying rate. Nor can you rely solely on factors that are easy to quantify, such as price, or simple to spot, such as beauty.

Inconveniently, the fact that you and I may dream about them can also have little to do with the final selection. In the final credits of my dreams I tend to find myself riding off towards the setting sun in an arthritic Escort, not some low-slung slice of ultimate auto-motive experience.

Most frustrating of all to someone charged with providing a list of the dreamiest cars of all time is that you can not rely on the simple truth that a car is great as a qualifying criterion. The Ford Mondeo is an undeniably great car, transforming the lot of the family on the move, but it has no more relevance to this book than does a bunch of bananas.

And you cannot even exclude cars that are genuinely bad to help narrow the field. In this book there is at least one car that even I consider to be truly dreadful and there are two or more others that when released received mixed reviews, to say the least. I will not be the first to observe that being bad can be a desirable trait.

In the end, then, it comes down to gut feeling and, in this case, my gut feeling. If you are lucky enough to have fluked your way into a business where driving such cars also earns you your living, you soon learn that this feeling, which manifests itself usually as a tingle in the pit of your stomach, is the most pre-cious tool of your trade. During the course of a year and perhaps a hundred car tests, you are routinely confronted with cars that, on paper, seem not to put a foot wrong but, out in the real world, fail to convince. Others seem to make no sense at all until you drive them and realize they possess a spark of something special that was not possible to predict. It is the ability to recognize and appreciate that spark that sets us apart from computers.

The next problem to be faced is that there are rather more candidates that fit comfortably into my gut's defintion of 'dream car' than there is space for in this book. To be honest, I could have filled it, cover to cover, with Ferraris without even drawing breath.

For me, as for millions around the globe, it was the Ferrari that lit the fire. My first memory of cars was being taken as a treat to the place where Ferraris are imported into the UK and sitting down surrounded by Daytonas and Dinos. I also remember the undig-nified exhibition I made of myself when it was suggested that perhaps it might be time to go home. I had never felt more at home in my life.

Of them all, it was the 250GTO that provided the first love and the feeling remains as strong today as ever. It was everything I had imagined a car should be: rare, indescribably beautiful, indomitable on the track and exquisite on the road. Blasting across open moorland while listening to the music of its classic

For me, as for millions around the globe, it was Ferrari that lit the fire.

V12 engine remains one of my all time great motoring experiences.

For a car that was, by comparison, mass produced, the Dino 246GT carried an unlikely amount of the GTO spirit. It looked almost as good and if it were not quite so quick, then it certainly sounded the part. Most importantly though, much of the Dino's desirability stems from the fact that, while not exactly on the cheap side, nor is it so ludicrously expensive that the prospect of ownership is beyond the grasp of all but a few dozen people on the planet.

The F40, however, is likely to remain out of reach, which, in fact, is no bad thing. It falls into that rare category of car that you cannot just climb aboard and, hoping you can handle it, head off over the hills. It is a car in which even the extremely experienced need to tread carefully. Once mastered, there is no other road car experience like it, but if the privilege is abused, there are few others on the road that will be as swift to punish the driver accordingly.

One of them, undoubtedly, is the Lancia Stratos, which, while not a Ferrari, at least relies on Ferrari for its power. The Stratos is an enigma, of all the cars I have driven, the most difficult to understand. Capable of being both merciless and endlessly rewarding, depending on its mood, it was one of the few road cars I remember approaching for the first time with a sense of fear. When driving it quickly in difficult conditions, you can never be truly certain what it was going to do next. Sometimes you would have a pretty strong hunch and act accordingly, but most of the time it was more a case of reacting.

Like the Stratos, the BMW M1 was conceived first as a competition car, from which road cars would be built to satisfy the prevailing regulations of the time. And while both were two-seater, mid-engined sportscars designed in the

1970s, the Stratos was built for the rally stage while the M1 was a racer, pure and simple. The road-going M1 made it onto the list because it was designed like an Italian supercar but built to the more exacting standards of a mainstream, quality German car maker. The theory was that the result would be a blend of style and function, and the practice agreed.

BMW turned to Lamborghini because, among other reasons, the Italian firm had been building mid-engined supercars for longer than anybody else. The first was the Miura, a car whose beauty and specification stunned the world when it was launched in 1966. Its memory lives on today as strong as ever in the Diablo SV. Lamborghini has never been idolized by its rivals at Ferrari, just twenty minutes down the road. Where Ferrari's competition history is unapproachable, that of Lamborghini is patchy and largely undistinguished; while Ferrari has raked in profits for year after year, Lamborghini has almost always struggled for survival. Yet whatever the future might hold for Lamborghini, it can face it rightly proud that, from the day the Miura first broke cover, it has never compromised its values.

But if there is one car that, alone, can claim not to have sold out to anyone from the day it was first produced, long before the Miura was on Bertone's drawing board, it is the Porsche 911. It has been in production for half a lifetime and its strengths are at least as valid today as they were in 1963. Yet from all those years of production, from the hundreds of model variants built in that time, just one stands alone as the definitive 911. It is the 2.7RS Carrera, born in 1973 and the progeny of a freakish alignment of all that ever was good in the 911. It is one of those rare cars that will tell you, after just a few miles at the wheel, that it is better than its makers could have ever intended.

The F1 is perhaps the only car that really has no competition.

The Porsche 959 was, strictly speaking, a 911 but one so far removed from the delicate sportscar from which it was derived that Porsche felt it best to rename it. Until the 959, despite certain claims at the time, no road car could come close to 320kph (200mph). A really good Lamborghini Countach might just reach 290kph (180mph), a 1984 Ferrari 288GTO was probably good for 303kph (188mph), though that was no higher than the speed Ferrari claimed for its Boxer back in 1971. But the 959 really would do 317kph (197mph) and with little fuss. Its crucial significance, though, is that without it we would never have seen the Ferrari F40 or the other 320-kph 200-mph) supercars that culminated, ultimately, in the 381-kph (237-mph) McLaren F1.

The F1 is perhaps the only car that really has no competition. Nothing can touch either its performance or price. Perhaps the best way to illustrate the commodity we are dealing with here is to promise you that the performance gap between the F1 and something really fast, such as a Ferrari 308GTB is much greater than that which exists between that 308 and a Mini. I spent three days with the F1, on test track, open road and runway. On the runway I found that, while some others might have a theoretical maximum of just over 320kph (200mph), if you held the McLaren at precisely that speed and then rammed your foot down, it would surge forward at a rate most others would be happy with at half that speed.

Back in 1907, the Rolls-Royce Silver Ghost was every bit as far ahead of the game as the McLaren F1. There was only one real Ghost, though others in its series were generally referred to as Silver Ghosts to honour its memory. Today it is very possibly the most valuable road car ever built, but that is not why it is in this book. It is here because

of its startling beauty and the quality and integrity of its design.

But Britain had to wait until the

Bentley was founded in 1919 before it could claim its first world-beating racing team. The marque won the Le Mans 24-hour race five times in seven attempts. If ever you wished to show an example of how classic lines could be achieved through pure function, you could do no better than use an open vintage Bentley as your illustration. Of them all, the most fondly remembered is the 4½-litre model.

It was not simply the slump and then the subsequent take-over by Rolls-Royce that signalled the end for Bentley. There was also some rather elegant Italian writing on the wall. It said "Alfa-Romeo 8C." It was one of the later breed of sportscars that acknowledged that you do not simply need ever larger engines to go faster. On the contrary, by cutting weight, smaller engines could be used to make the car go just as fast in a straight line while reducing the effort required both to make the car stop and to go around a corner. The result was a car that was complete in every area, one that would go, stop and

It is here because of its startling beauty and the quality and integrity of its design.

The ultimate modern expression of all that is Mercedes can be found within the skin of the 500SL roadster.

steer with the best of them while featuring the sort of effortless style of which only the Italians seem really capable.

The Aston Martin DB7 uses a supercharged engine, too, utilizing once more an often neglected form of induction. But that is not the feature that will ensure that it is remembered for generations to come. The DB7 is the vehicle that saved the company, a backs-to-the-wall last-gasp triumph that not only secured the Aston's future until the 21st century but also sent it on its way with greater confidence than at any stage in its heroically fraught history. But even if the DB7 was less than brilliant, you would still find it in this book. Its styling is the work of absolute genius. It is not a question of simple good looks, it is the way those looks both look forward to the future while still honouring the heritage of Aston Martin.

And none is better at defining that heritage than the famous DB5. It had all those things without which no Aston Martin is complete: speed, style, beautiful quality and still a certain brutality to its nature.

Its biggest rival was the Jaguar E-type. Jaguar had built its reputation on making cars that were both faster and cheaper than its erstwhile rivals but the E-type was something else again. Even now, there are those who feel that the original 3.8 litre coupé captured the essence of the sportscar better than any other. Certainly it was stunning to look at, comparatively inexpensive and, if not quite capable of the top speed claimed for it, it was nevertheless much faster than

anything else the money would buy.

Honda might not be a name to make you swoon but the NSX showed the world that there was no area of automative endeavor in which the Japanese could not excel. A technological masterpiece, constructed to breathtaking standards from aluminium and powered by an engine that actually used pure technology not to replace emotive feel, but to create it. And anyone who tells you that an NSX is a sterile, emotionless experience to drive has not driven one properly.

These, then, are those that make up the first division. They are the icons, the cars that have either already attained the status of legends or will shortly do so. Do not, however, think that this knowledge should detract from those that follow.

Mercedes enters the reckoning for the first time with two cars separated by 35 years. The ultimate modern expression of all that is Mercedes can be found within the skin of the 500SL roadster. Beautiful but, above all, effective, this is a ground coverer by day that also guarantees you a seat in the right restaurant by night.

It is related back to the original 300SL a car that, in 1955, was years ahead of its time, offering speed in a package as civilized and utterly reliable as you

would expect from any car wearing the three pointed star. It started life in 1952 as an extremely successful sports racing car but it was as a road car that it found fame.

The Ford GT40 also started life as a racing car, and proved so successful it is a wonder that anybody bothered making them for use on the road. The road-going GT40, or MkIII, should never have been built. What is incredible about it, though, is the way that first-hand knowledge of how truly bad it is fails to diminish its magic. Just to sit in one so scarcely removed from a car that won Le Mans four times is reason enough to make it achingly desirable.

One car that would turn heads more would be the GT40's fellow American, the Chrysler Viper GTS. And unlike so many great-looking American cars built since the oil crisis of the seventies, the mechanicals of the Viper more than keep the promise of its looks. Its ten-cylinder motor displaces no less than eight litres, making it the biggest power plant fitted to a car on sale around the world. The Viper's real charm, however, is that it is straightforward to the point of crudeness, a real American muscle car and all the better for it.

Lamborghini re-enters the fray with a couple of latter-day lunatics–the Diablo SV and Countach QV. Drive either and you will find a considerable chunk of the original Miura concept in the cabin. There may not be a single interchangeable part, but in their noise,

their lack of practicality and heavy feel they are inextricably linked in a way that Ferrari could not credibly claim existed between its latest 550 Maranello and the car it produced to fight the Miura, the 365GTB/4 Daytona.

Jaguar has further entries. They star with the XK120, the car that, through speed and beauty, put the Coventry firm in the hearts and minds of the post-war world, where it has remained ever since. By comparison few will have ever heard of the XKSS, a little known road-going version of the all conquering D-type racing car. Only a handful were made but within its flowing lines lay the template for the E-type, the greatest road-going Jaguar of all.

It would be more than 30 years before Jaguar built another car with as great a performance advantage over the opposition as the E-type. It was called the XJ220 and, given enough space, would wind itself up to 343kph (213mph). As you will read, there was much that was wrong with the 220 but, like the E-type before, its looks and performance earned it a great deal of forgiveness. It was the first car that said, unequivocally, that 320kph (200mph) was not enough. And now Jaguar is back to its winning ways once more with the XK8. Hailed around the world as the best Jaguar for a generation, it has the looks and punch not only to back this claim but also to re-establish the marque as one of the premier sports

That honour belongs to the Elise, which is just about the most breathtaking, affordable sportscar you can buy.

These are cars to uplift the spirit when one howls past.

coupé maunfacturers.

Another is Bentley. This great name, once reduced to being no more than Rolls-Royce Silver Shadows with different badges, is ascending once more and it is largely thanks to the Continental R–a sporting coupé in the finest tradition. Thanks to its speed and lines it has helped turn the company around, and Bentley now out-produces Rolls-Royce.

Lotus is another name recently back from the dead. In fact, the survival of the road cars has depended entirely on the Esprit of late and there is none finer to represent this marvellous breed than the exclusive Sport 300. It was not, however, the car that turned it all around for the marque. That honour belongs to the Elise, which is just about the most breathtaking, affordable sportscar you can buy.

But not quite. The Caterham Seven JPE claims that one for itself, and with it the title of most frightening road car ever built. It has been developed from the old world Lotus Seven into a car that would need another the calibre of a McLaren to stay with it across country or, more advisedly, around a racetrack.

Ferrari wades back into the second division with four cars that prove its unparalleled depth and breadth of excellence. From the history books comes the 288GTO–a flawed car but, in its day, faster and more wild than anything else you could buy. There are faster cars than an F50 or F355, Ferrari's contemporary contenders, but not many. These are cars to uplift the spirit when one howls past. If you are ever lucky enough to travel in one, you will know, within a mile, what it is that makes these cars different.

Snapping at their heels, as ever, come the Porsches, two of our contenders in the second division representing the marque's now generation-old front-engined models. First comes the 928GT,

not quite the ultimate but undoubtedly the best development of the original 928 concept that won the Car of the Year award back in 1978. And if that seems like an age ago, remember that the car that sired the sublime 968 Club Sport was the 924, which you could buy way back in 1975. Say what you like about Porsche, you cannot deny that it builds its cars to last. The 356 Speedster, however, is not here for traditional Porsche reasons. Its presence within these pages is to show that Porsche could achieve the truly beautiful as well as the fast and enduring.

Just two hours down the road from Porsche lies the Munich base of BMW, and its three contenders in this section bear witness to the amazing breadth of sportscars produced by this enigmatic marque. How could a car such as the mad 2002Turbo, with its wild body-work and all-or-nothing engine response, have ever come from the same company that brought you the Z1, as sophisticated a junior roadster as has been seen until the Mercedes SLK. Finally, the Bavarians bring us the 3.0CSL, known in bewinged racing form as the Batmobile.

An hour North of BMW lies Ingolstadt, home of Audi. When it produced the Quattro in 1980, nobody knew it would become the most significant sportscar of the decade. It was not very pretty and it had some damning flaws, but in its use of four-wheel drive for an every-day road coupé, it was unique and its influence on the cars we drive today would be hard to overestimate.

The American presence in this part of the book is not limited just to the Chrysler Viper and Ford GT40. Indeed, you will find the same engine Ford used for the GT40 under the bonnet of the AC Cobra, an Anglo/American hybrid of legendary appearance and unforget-table performance. Chrysler, too, is not finished yet, and puts forward its formidable Dodge Charger–as purebred an example of the straight-forward American muscle-car breed as you will find. And the last member of the Big Three, General Motors, makes it into the final reckoning, albeit with a little help from Lotus. The Chevrolet Corvette ZR1 was the first of its type to move as well as it looked, thanks to the engineering expertise of the British firm. It stands tall as easily the finest of America's most famous breed of sportscar.

You might find it hard to see how a maker of such mainstream and often humble cars as Renault could find a place in a book such as this. If so, you have surely forgotten their mid-engined masterpiece–the Renault Five Turbo–a car that indeed looked like a Renault Five yet, despite using a tiny engine of undistinguished origin, was capable of running rings around many of the supercars of the day.

The Alfa-Romeo Montreal should have been able to do the same. It did, after all, harbour the engine of an all-out racing car within its gorgeous lines. The fact that the result was frequently and curiously awful in no way compromises its right to be included within this book.

Aston Martin's final two contenders represent the poles of the marque's post-war design. First, there is the Zagato–a brutal styling exercise by the famous Italian coachbuilders whose name it

bears. To date, nobody has ever called the result pretty but the performance from the tuned V8 Vantage engine was never in doubt.

The DB2/4 MkIII could scarcely be more different. It is a beautiful, elegant sportscar from a time before James Bond, and its appeal is as subtle as it is real.

Finally come the TVR Cerbera and the Lister Storm, both the progeny of Britain's tiny, but determined, specialist sportscar industry. They are monstrously fast two-plus-two coupés as individual as those who drive them. But while the Cerbera is beautiful and 'affordable', the Storm's shape owes much to aerodynamic efficiency and little to subtle styling nuances.

In this book there is a selection of marques from three continents, six countries and 90 years of car production. The difference in top speed between fastest and slowest is 290kph (180mph), while the price gap is rather more than £600,000, or about $1 million. And because this means that the net has been cast far and wide there are sure to be some entrants you will feel have no right to be included, and perhaps rather more than have been excluded.

I make no apology for this. If it is any comfort, there were another 50 on a shortlist that did not make it. One day, I might attempt to do justice to them as well, as I hope I have done with this selection. Until then, I am afraid that this modest little assortment will have to suffice.

Ferrari F40

The F40 had perhaps the meanest shape of all. On first acquaintance, it is not at all beautiful but after a while its sheer sense of purpose becomes utterly compelling.

It was the last road car Enzo Ferrari ever saw and, fittingly, it remains the fastest ever built by his factory. Sure, today's F50 has more power and, arguably, the higher top speed, but for sheer acceleration the later car's extra weight means it cannot conceivably keep up with its parent.

The F40 is an enigma. In its day, ten years ago, it was the fastest thing that had ever been let out in public – a car that, in standard form, would crack 97kph (60mph) in less than 4 seconds and carry you right up to the door of 322kph (200mph). And this was only the opening bid. Pay the price and Ferrari would fit bigger turbochargers to its 2.8-litre, V8 motor – an act that, in a trice, put up the power output from 478bhp to something around 650bhp.

More than any other supercar, more even than the leather-lined McLaren F1, the F40 feels like a racing car. You climb in over a wide, carbon-fibre sill (from which the car is clad, not constructed) and settle down in a thin racing seat and fasten up the racing harness. The door clangs shut, revealing just a strip of wire across its frame, which is the handle. Ahead lies a suede-covered, three-spoke racing wheel, with the yellow Ferrari emblem at its centre, and simple white-on-black instruments beyond. Turn the key and you will hear nothing but the whir of fuel pumps. To start an F40, you need to press a button, too.

It is a deeply intimidating car to drive, and it's not simply the snarling from the scarcely silenced motor that prises your

heart loose from its moorings and sends it bobbing into your throat. The clutch is heavy and unforgiving and, driven at even normal traffic speeds, there is so much banging and crashing from the racing suspension that any hopes of a remotely civilized run flee the mind in seconds.

Find the right road – and there are few of these indeed where the F40 can be exercised both properly and safely – and you will discover a driving experience more intense even than that provided by the undoubtedly quicker McLaren F1. At first the engine seems a little sluggish, pulling slowly from idle up to around 3,000rpm before a banshee wail, as the turbochargers gather speed, heralds one of the most explosive deployments of power the car industry has ever produced.

Unlike the McLaren, which goes hard at all engine speeds, the F40 saves it up for one even bigger bang – the rev-counter needle doesn't seem to swing around to the red line; it just appears there. The noise is deafening and quite beautiful, and the rate of progress up the road truly surreal to all

who have not sampled such performance before. It makes all conventionally fast supercars seem truly impotent.

Through it all, what you will not suspect until you really know its ways is that this most ferocious of all supercars is, in fact, on your side. Many miles teach you to

Compared with the F40, the F512M (above) was a softer and altogether more civilized machine. Compared with almost anything else, it was simply staggering.

Previous page: The F40 was Enzo Ferrari's last road car and, for the author at least, his finest.

Twin Behr intercoolers dominate the engine bay. They run through two Japanese IHI turbos to provide the most exciting experience of any supercar built.

The cabin is that of a stripped-out racer. Note the carbon-fibre panelling and drawstring for opening the doors.

push a little harder, looking for that first manifestation of devilry. It never comes. As long as you choose the right roads, those that are safe, open, dry and deserted, the F40 will show you things that you thought no car could do – least of all one driven by you.

It is a uniquely intimate and an intense driving experience, all the better for the final realization that what lies at the edge of it (and your abilities) is not the oblivion you had suspected but perhaps, instead, the finest driving experience of them all.

Ferrari F40

Manufactured: 1987-91
Number of cars: 1,100

Dimensions
Length: 4,358mm
Width: 1,970mm
Height: 1,124mm
Wheelbase: 2,450mm
Front track/rear track: n/a
Kerb weight: 1,235kg

Engine
Capacity: 2,936cc
Bore/stroke: 82mm/70mm
Construction: Aluminium head,
 aluminium block
Valve gear: 4 valves per cylinder, dohc
Compression ratio: 7.7:1
Max power: 478bhp at 7,000rpm
Max torque: 425lb ft at 4,000rpm
Gearbox: 5-speed manual

Brakes
Front: Ventilated discs
Rear: Ventilated discs
Servo assistance/anti-lock: Yes/no

Suspension
Front: Double wishbones, coil springs,
 anti-roll bar
Rear: Double wishbones, coil springs,
 anti-roll bar

Steering system
Unassisted rack and pinion

Wheels and tyres
Wheel size: 8.0 x 17in (f), 13.0 x 17in (r)
Construction: Alloy
Tyre size: 245/40 ZR 17 (f), 335/35 ZR 17 (r)

Claimed performance
0-97kph (0-60mph): 4.1sec
Max speed: 323kph (201mph)

The F40 was not simply a car you could go out and buy if you had enough money. Following the precedent set by its father, the 288GTO, Ferrari decided to offer the F40 only to a few of its most valued clients. This, and the fact that Ferrari made it quite clear that it would frown on any attempt by owners to sell their cars on for a quick profit, made their value on the second-hand market during the boom-time at the end of the 1980s rocket skywards from less than £200,000 to amounts in excess of £300,000.

Perhaps the most famous F40 owner is Nick Mason – Pink Floyd's drummer and a rabid car enthusiast. Mason does not buy his cars for traditional rock-star reasons but because he feels that they are there to be driven. Consequently, the F40 has made regular appearances on the pages of magazines all over the world and continues to be driven hard to this day. Other F40s have been owned or driven by all of Ferrari's top drivers, such as Nigel Mansell, Alain Prost and Gerhard Berger, while Gordon Murray, the designer of the McLaren F1 is a well-known fan.

The hardest driven of all, however, are the racing F40s. Like the McLaren F1, the F40 was not designed as a racing car and it was some years before the prevailing regulations made the most of its latent talents. Now, however, the true potential of the F40 has been realized – sadly some ten years after the car was first released. Even so, despite being considerably older than its rivals, the F40 has competed at the highest levels, winning races against uniformly younger opposition in global sportscar racing.

Ferraris have never been cars to be taken lightly and more than one F40 has caught out an inexperienced driver. Luckily, the one above is being driven by Nigel Mansell and is midway through about a dozen impeccably controlled gyrations.

Nigel Mansell enjoyed driving F40s during his time as a Grand Prix driver for Ferrari. His favourite trick was the 'doughnut', the results of which can be seen on the left.

Bentley 4½ litre

Just half an hour in a vintage Bentley is all you need to dispel, for all time, any idea that cars built during the 1920s were simply lame old crocks that spend at least half their time holding up the traffic and the remainder as steaming and stranded monuments to the folly of their owners' aspirations. True, most cars built during this era were not reliable in the way that we simply take for granted these days, nor were they capable of much more than about 65kph (40mph). But the Bentleys were not like this.

The vintage Bentley is a real powerhouse and, in its day, it was capable of travelling further and faster than any other motor vehicle on the planet. This is attested to by its four consecutive victories in the gruelling Le Mans 24-hour race.

Bentleys came in all shapes and sizes, from little 3-litre tourers to massive 8-litre limousines. But of them all, the one that is most fondly remembered and, today, tends to be the hardest driven, is the 4½-litre model. This was the car that best combined the relative agility of the smaller models with quite a sizeable chunk of the performance of the larger-engined, heavier, six-cylinder Bentleys.

And because this model had only four cylinders, each one displacing more than a litre, once heard the noise of the engine is unforgettable – an impossibly deep, thumping thunder that shakes you to the very core of your soul.

Many people think that such technological advances as four-valves per cylinder, an overhead camshaft and twin-spark ignition are entirely modern phenomena. In fact, when the initial Bentley prototype first fired up in a Cricklewood yard in London back in 1919, it – like every other vehicle produced until 1931, the year of the company's liquidation – came so equipped.

Even the 3-litre engine produced startling performance for its time, but it was the 4½-litre Bentley that first started to knock regularly on the door of that magical 160kph (100mph), a speed that, incidentally, feels not dissimilar to about 260kph (160mph) in a modern car.

But the key to the magic of this Bentley is not its speed. To be honest, a modest Ford Fiesta would have little trouble drawing away from the 4½ today. No, it is not the

speed itself – it is the nature of that speed that provides one of the most stirring drives of any car, from any era, and at any price.

The cockpit is dominated by a huge, Bakelite steering wheel with Jaeger instruments dotted around the dashboard. Look down at your feet and you soon realize that the accelerator is the one in the middle (the brake is on the right). The race-bred gearbox has no synchromesh at all, which means that perfect matches of engine to gear ratio speed are required for every change simply to persuade the gear lever to engage the next ratio. Even if you are going to drive it slowly, you are going to be busy.

Out on the road, driving hard, you soon lose your own identity and simply become

Overleaf: The heart of any Bentley is the engine. This model has just four cylinders, each one displacing more than a litre. Properly looked after, they tend to go on for ever.

This, believe it or not, is a Bentley prepared for Le Mans, which the marque won five times. At the wheel is Frank Clement, the only professional racing driver in the team.

Bentley 4½ litre

Manufactured: 1927-30
Number of cars: 665

Dimensions
Length: 4,381mm
Width: 1,740mm
Height: 1,245mm
Wheelbase: 3,302mm
Front track/rear track: 1,270mm/1,270mm
Kerb weight: 1,651kg

Engine
Capacity: 4,398cc
Bore/stroke: 100mm/140mm
Construction: Cast-iron, head in block
Valve gear: 4 valves per cylinder, sohc
Compression ratio: n/a
Max power: 110bhp at 3,500rpm
Max torque: n/a
Gearbox: 4-speed manual

Brakes
Front: Drums
Rear: Drums
Servo assistance/anti-lock: No/no

Suspension
Front: Beam axle, semi-elliptic longitudinal
    leaf springs
Rear: Live axle, semi-elliptic longitudinal
    leaf springs

Steering system
Unassisted worm and wheel

Wheels and tyres
Wheel size: 5.25 x 21in
Construction: Steel, spoked
Tyre size: 5.25 x 21in

Claimed performance
0-97kph (0-60mph): 13sec (estimated)
Max speed: 148kph (92mph)

Beautiful knock-on wire wheels carry spinners bearing
the name of the marque and a reminder that, until 1931,
Bentleys were produced in Cricklewood, North London.

Opposite: A massive steering wheel is essential since a
Bentley is not light on its feet. Classic Jaeger instruments are all over the dash. A Bentley is not the easiest
car to drive thanks to the accelerator being to the left
of the brake.

that part of the car that coordinates its different functions, from steering to gears to pedals. Every driving action requires an input that is as solid and as heavy as the car while, as the speeds increase, your senses are brutally assaulted by the rushing wind, the throbbing engine and the gear-whine, and you are shaken and shuddered by every pockmark and change of level on the road surface that makes it past the mercilessly stiff suspension.

In a lesser car, such a physical battering could become a misery for the driver; in the Bentley 4½, however, your efforts and endurance are amply rewarded by a sense of pure elation at journey's end that few cars, even among the marvels in this book, could ever hope to produce. It is an elation born from a car that requires total commitment on the part of the driver and provides, in return, sensations more intense and in tune with those who demand total involvement than just about any other. The result is one of the greatest cars ever built.

The story of the Bentley Boys is just as fascinating as that of the cars they raced with such panache. Having survived the Great War, these characters lived life for the moment, and to the full. Most famous among them was Sir Henry 'Tim' Birkin, the most fearless racer of his era and the creator of the legendary Blower Bentley. His finest hour came when, during the 1930 Le Mans race, he overtook the leading 7.2-litre Mercedes in his 4½-litre Bentley while travelling at nearly 210kph (130mph). At the time he was on the grass with a rear tyre in tatters. The Mercedes driver was not fussed, since he realized that the Bentley would have to pull into the pits to replace the tyre. Birkin, however, had other ideas about this and, on the next lap, broke the track record.

The real saviour of the company was, however, a gentleman called Woolf Barnato. A diamond millionaire, playboy extraordinaire and all round sportsman, he was chairman of the company, supported its flagging finances until 1931 and once, for a bet, raced the famous Blue Train from the south of France to London, winning with ease despite having to arrange fuel supplies along the route. History shows that he entered the Le Mans 24-hour race on just three consecutive occasions and won every one of them – a record of achievement that stands unchallenged to this day.

Today, vintage Bentleys are campaigned vigorously all over the world by the likes of Prince Michael of Kent, ex-Aston Martin chairman Victor Gauntlett and the world's leading dealer of the marque, Stanley Mann. Thanks to their bomb-proof, indestructible engineering and the spirit of the Bentley Boys that burns as brightly today as ever in those that drive them competitively, they can be relied on not simply to finish any given event but usually to do so before any other competitor.

Opposite: Bentleys hunt in packs to this day, usually competing in the classic road trials such as the 1,600-km (1,000-mile) Mille Miglia retrospective from Brescia in northern Italy to Rome and back.

Ferrari 250GTO

People used to say that Ferrari built you an engine and threw in the rest of the car for free. On the road, the GTO proved them all wrong: it handles as well as any from its era.

It was one of those shapes that just happened, created from a desire to disturb the wind as little as possible while moving through it at about 290kph (180mph). It was the desire that created the Ferrari 250GTO.

There was nothing particularly clever about the GTO. A simple chassis with independent front suspension and semi-elliptic leaf springs at the back, which looked pretty old hat even back in 1962. The engine, too, was by no means in the first flush – a further development of the 3-litre, V12 Colombo-designed motor that had powered the Testa Rossa back in 1958, itself just one more iteration of a design that could be traced back further still.

But it worked. It gave Enzo Ferrari the most successful GT racer of the early 1960s: for the rest of us, perhaps the most beautiful and enigmatic road car of all time. Enzo never did give a damn about his road cars.

On even the most beautiful cars, there is usually one angle where its lines look less than completely comfortable. On the GTO, this angle does not exist. Above all, it looks effortlessly attractive, as if no human hand could actively have contrived to create a shape so natural.

Inside, the race car origins are obvious. Doors are opened by tugging on a bit of wire strung across the frame, while speedometers are fitted only to those of the 39 built that require them for use on the public roads.

Ferrari guaranteed that all GTO engines would produce between 296 and 302bhp, giving an approximate specific output of 100bhp per litre – an achievement that would not be repeated by a normally aspirated road car engine for more than 30 years. Yet, despite all of this, the V12 is docile, easy to start and flexible across its 8,000rpm rev-range.

By modern standards it is still quick, its outright performance being impossible to determine for certain, thanks to the myriad axle ratios that Ferrari offered. Certainly, however, a GTO has covered the 0-97kph (0-60mph) sprint in under 6 seconds and, since it weighs scarcely more than a tonne, such a figure is bound to be conservative.

What matters rather more than the exact size of the GTO's performance envelope is its quality. It is this that has had all who have been lucky enough to sit behind that huge wooden wheel in raptures. The noise is exquisite, an unfettered symphony from the days before legislation started to stifle engines and exhausts. It seems that every sound, from the thrash of the chains driving the single camshaft on each bank of the engine to the regimented suckings of the six, twin-choke carburettors, can be singled out and its contribution to the overall song clearly identified. As the revs rise, the note changes from a snarl to a howl to a scream just before the next gear is demanded and, with a slam of the hand, joyously provided.

It handles better than you would imagine, too, providing a millimetre-perfect guide to conditions underfoot through chassis and steering, complete with the balance and agility to give the driver the confidence to push that little bit harder. And the harder you drive it, the better it feels.

Most cars in this book have singular talents to explain their appeal. The GTO is not one of them. Its appeal is founded on all fronts, from performance and handling to its looks. It is perhaps this that explains why the GTO holds the record for the highest price ever paid for a car – a reputed £10 million back in 1989.

Overleaf: A GTO parked outside an amusement arcade in the north of England. No one should need telling which one provides the bigger buzz.

Was there ever a more beautiful car? Many would say not. There is not a bad line on the car nor an angle from which it looks less than exquisite.

ART CENTER
COLLEGE LIBRARY

3 GTO

If you needed convincing that the beauty was more than skin deep, look at this Colombo-designed V12 taken from the Testa Rossa sports racer and tuned to produce 300 totally reliable horsepower from just three litres. Not bad for 1962.

The cabin of the GTO is that of a stark racer, and the speedometer an afterthought, tacked on behind the gear lever to make the car road legal. The instrument that dominates the dashboard is the rev-counter.

Ferrari 250GTO

Manufactured: 1962-63
Number of cars: 39

Dimensions
Length: 4,400mm
Width: 1,675mm
Height: 1,245mm
Wheelbase: 2,595mm
Front track/rear track: 1,351mm/1,346mm
Kerb weight: 1,078kg

Engine
Capacity: 2,953cc
Bore/stroke: 73mm/59mm
Construction: Aluminium head, cast-iron block
Valve gear: 2 valves per cylinder, sohc
Compression ratio: 9.7:1
Max power: 300bhp at 7,800rpm
Max torque: 253lb ft at 5,500rpm
Gearbox: 5-speed manual

Brakes
Front: Ventilated discs
Rear: Ventilated discs
Servo assistance/anti-lock: No/no

Suspension
Front: Double wishbones, coil springs,
   anti-roll bar
Rear: Trailing arms, leaf springs,
   anti-roll bar

Steering system
Unassisted recirculating ball

Wheels and tyres
Wheel size: 6.0 x 15in (f), 7.0 x 15in (r)
Construction: Steel, spoked
Tyre size: 6.0 x 15in (f), 7.0 x 15in (r)

Claimed performance
0-97kph (0-60mph): 5.9sec
Max speed: 241kph (150mph) plus

Just 39 GTOs were built, although some people claim that a 40th exists. From the outset, they were raced by the finest drivers of the time, including Innes Ireland, Jack Sears and Mike Parkes.

Today, Ferrari GTOs are still raced with vigour at classic motorsports meetings, none more so than that owned by the Pink Floyd drummer Nick Mason. Readily identified by its '250GTO' number plate, this is one of the most famous and well-used examples in the world. Nor is it kept exclusively for track use. It is actively campaigned on the road in historical retro-spectives throughout Europe, while once, when freezing weather conditions meant that none of the modern cars in the Mason stable would start, the children were taken to school in the GTO.

Sir Anthony Bamford, of JCB digger fame, has two GTOs, one of the earlier and more familiar shape and another of the later, and no less lovely, 1964 iteration, which has been raced with considerable success by the fearless historic and contem-porary racing-car driver and BMW Alpina agent, Frank Sytner.

Thanks to its fame, beauty and heritage, a huge business has sprung up creating lookalikes running on rather more humble mechanicals than the original. Ferrari takes a deeply dim view of all such cars but, as long as their creators make no reference to Ferrari or the model they are attempting to imitate, either in their literature or on the cars, there is little Ferrari can do to stop it. Those who have mentioned or alluded to the Ferrari name have, very often, been sued on the spot.

Despite this, there are now many more cars that look like GTOs than were ever built so, if you see one across the street, don't get run over in the rush to pore over it – it is probably a fake.

Opposite: The racing fuel filler is now seen as a thing of beauty. When it was designed, it was simply the quickest way to refuel the car during a race.

Tail down, accelerating hard away from another corner, this is the GTO in its element. On the road, it was probably the best racing car ever built.

Porsche 911 2.7RS Carrera

The stories tell you that you can't slide an old 911 safely in public. The above proves that the stories are nonsense. Treated well, this 911 will not bite anyone.

Nobody, least of all Porsche, could have predicted the success of the 911. Indeed, for a sizeable part of its life, Porsche itself had directed its not inconsiderable resources towards killing it, and still failed. Incredibly, the Porsche 928, introduced in 1978, was planned from the outset to replace the 911. The 928's production life finally ended after 17 successful years; the 911 continues undaunted.

The finest of all, oddly, was neither the very first nor the very latest. Nor was it the fastest nor most expensive version. It was the 2.7RS Carrera, manufactured for only a short time in 1973, that was to become known as the definitive template for the breed, the one to whose standards all the others aspired.

Drive one and it is easy to see why. Conceived by a desire to keep the 911 at the forefront of road-car-based GT racing, there was nothing particularly clever about its design compared with other 911s. The magic was in the execution. The programme was simple: to make the 911 go faster it would become both lighter and more powerful. The air-cooled, flat-six, 2.4-litre engine was stretched to 2.7 litres and tuned to produce a rousing 210bhp. Suspension and brakes were modified to accommodate the extra urge, while every single unnecessary item of interior trim was removed in the interests of saving weight. Lightweight body panels were fitted and even the glass in the windows was specially commissioned to be lighter and thinner than that found in a standard 911.

On the road, the RS provides an object lesson in the art of harmonizing man with machine. Every mile is a revelation in communication, driving involvement and satisfaction. The engine, freed from stifling noise-deadening material, sounds urgent in a way that's missing from 911s today. It also revs to 7,200rpm, a speed at which no production 911 engine is allowed to turn these days. It is also faster than a modern 911, for although the older engine may lack the outright power of the much larger units employed today, so they lack the RS's trim waistline, which more than makes up the difference.

Best of all, though, is the handling. This 911 dates from the days when reams of nonsense was written by those who should have known better giving the 911 an only

partially deserved reputation for malevolent handling. An RS, however, is just not like this. As long as you treat it with the respect it deserves, it will not let you down in the toughest of situations. Quite the reverse, it will reward your efforts with sensations through the steering and chassis that mark it out to be one of the all time great sportscars and, with its unique ducktail spoiler and clean lines, one of the prettiest.

All the above would earn the RS its place in this book and its most outstanding talent has yet to be mentioned. What really made the RS special among the tiny handful of Ferraris and Lamborghinis that stood a chance of keeping up with it on a tricky road was that not only did it cost a fraction of the price, you could also use it as an everyday car for year after year and it would never go wrong. It's reliability was near total and it didn't matter whether you used it to sit in traffic jams all day or race it around tracks, it was just about unbreakable. If there was one car that should carry the credit for the on-going proliferation of the 911 legend, the 2.7RS Carrera is it.

Overleaf: By even the standards of today, a lightweight 911 is a rather rapid device. Back in 1973, however, it would have been unlike almost anything then seen on the public road.

A Carrera working hard on the roads of Wales' Brecon Beacons. These are the conditions you need before the 2.7RS will reveal its awesome soul.

The magical flat-six engine uses air, not water, to keep cool, hence the huge fan. The engine made its debut with the car in 1963 and it lasted until the end of 1997.

The instruments have hardly changed over the years and the rev-counter is still the dominating feature. The big steering wheel shows the car's age.

Porsche 911 2.7RS Carrera

Manufactured: 1973
Number of cars: 1,579

Dimensions
Length: 4,102mm
Width: 1,652mm
Height: 1,320mm
Wheelbase: 2,271mm
Front track/rear track: 1,372mm/1,368mm
Kerb weight: 960kg

Engine
Capacity: 2,687cc
Bore/stroke: 90mm/70mm
Construction: Aluminium head,
   aluminium block
Valve gear: 2 valves per cylinder, sohc
Compression ratio: 8.5:1
Max power: 210bhp at 6,300rpm
Max torque: 188lb ft at 5,100rpm
Gearbox: 5-speed manual

Brakes
Front: Ventilated discs
Rear: Ventilated discs
Servo assistance/anti-lock: Yes/no

Suspension
Front: McPherson struts, torsion bar
   springing, anti-roll bar
Rear: Semi-trailing arms, torsion bar
   springing, anti-roll bar

Steering system
Unassisted rack and pinion

Wheels and tyres
Wheel size: 6.0 x 15in (f), 7.0 x 15in (r)
Construction: Alloy
Tyre size: 165/70 VR 15 (f), 185/70 VR 15 (r)

Claimed performance
0-97kph (0-60mph): 5.8sec
Max speed: 245kph (152mph)

Racing seats for the 911 are not standard but they are more than welcome, and the no-nonsense cabin is still very practical and roomy for two. While the lack of sound-deadening material makes it raucous, it is not an unpleasant companion on a long run.

The versatility of the Porsche 911 knows almost no bounds. As happy when sitting in traffic as being flogged around a race track, in one form or another the 911 has won every event – from the most gruelling on the track, the Le Mans 24-hours, to the most arduous on the road, the legendary Paris-Dakar rally. They became part of the staple diet of racing drivers around the world for their unrivalled ability to deliver you to the track on time while still providing a stimulating challenge on the way. Look at the Steve McQueen film *Le Mans* and see which car he chose to drive when out of the racer . . . inevitably it was a 911.

The bombproof mechanicals also meant that the 911 was more susceptible than most to the attentions of the independent tuner. The acknowledged master of this art is the German tuning house RUF, which churns out entirely rebuilt 911s with power considerably in excess of 500bhp.

The actual RS version's racing successes continued for many years after it should have become technically obsolete. I remember watching a race at Brands Hatch in terrible weather full of shining new Porsches with smart liveries, bulging bodywork and even turbocharged engines. I watched as they slithered and slipped their way around the circuit while, way out in front, two slightly tatty 2.7RS Carreras simply disappeared from the rest of the uniformly younger pack.

Fans of the RS are far and wide and, it would seem, they have found true soulmates in the McLaren Formula One drivers who latterly earned their living as commentators once their front-line racing days were over: both Ulsterman John Watson and the late and much missed James Hunt owned, drove and enjoyed 2.7RS Carreras, as did Hunt's team owner in his earlier Formula One days, Lord Hesketh.

Opposite: The duck-tail spoiler was once the best way to tell an RS from a normal 911. Sadly, there are so many good and bad imitations around now that it is just as likely to be seen on a fake as the real thing.

The basic 911 shape, without all of the safety-orientated clutter of later years, is clearly more beautiful: some would call it a true work of automotive art.

McLaren F1

The McLaren shape was defined by what would create the best airflow over the body and then styled to create a car of considerable beauty and no little presence.

Opposite (both): To date there has never been a faster car built for the public road and, it has been suggested, there never will be. Who needs to do more than 380kph (237mph)?

There is a strong argument to suggest that the McLaren F1 is the most remarkable car ever built. Unlike every other car made today, its design benefited not just from a blank sheet of paper, but also from a blank chequebook.

First it was crafted entirely from carbon-fibre, the most expensive, strongest and lightest building material employed in the car industry, and then screwed together to aircraft-quality standards. The BMW company was commissioned to produce the most powerful production road car engine in history – a 6.1-litre, V12 powerhouse pumping out 627bhp – while sheets of 24-carat gold were used to reflect its heat for no other reason than that gold is the best heat reflector in the world.

The driver sits in the middle, but this is no racing car. It seats three instead of the more usual two, has air conditioning, leather upholstery, perhaps the finest stereo system ever fitted to a car and ample space for your luggage.

Under full power, the acceleration is actually uncomfortable up to around 240kph (150mph). The fact that it will reach 160kph (100mph) in 6.3 seconds, an extremely swift 0-97kph (0-60mph) time for most sportscars, is, in fact, one of the less extraordinary facts surrounding the McLaren's performance. More compelling is the news that it will accelerate from 160-320kph (100-200mph), which is much faster than most can manage 0-160kph (0-100mph). At 290kph (180mph) it still has a gear to go, and at 320kph (200mph) it is really starting to get into its stride.

It is a car that moves you from one place to another seemingly by leaving out the bit in the middle, one where the searing howl of the V12 motor blends with your frenzied

gear changes as you hurtle to the horizon to create an unparalleled automotive assault on your senses. Exit a corner, put your foot down and, before you have had time to think about anything other than changing gear twice, you will be doing 257kph (160mph), a speed at which it will explode forward like most supercars do from rest.

And yet, so sophisticated is its design, so docile its engine that the F1 can be driven to the shops, sat in traffic until the tank runs dry and prove no more difficult to drive than any other car. If you restricted the accelerator to a quarter of its movement and its engine to 3,000rpm, anyone with a licence could safely drive an F1.

Unleashed, though, and it is a car that will bite – and it has bitten even some extremely experienced drivers. There is nothing fundamentally wrong with the chassis, indeed it is one of the greats, but with traction control, four-wheel drive and anti-lock brakes all ruled out in pursuit of lightness, all that power needs applying extremely carefully in anything less than ideal conditions.

Sadly, although the F1 was one of the two or three most exciting road cars ever constructed, it will not be remembered as a success in that role. Originally slanted for a production run of 350, less than a hundred were finally built, killed off by

Previous page: The XP5 motif on the flank reveals this to be the fifth and final experimental proto-type before the tiny production run started.

This shot has not been faked. The McLaren is being driven at 340kph (211mph) at a proving ground. It did 0-320kph (0-200mph) in 28 seconds.

the potential customers who walked away, no longer prepared to spend whatever it took to have the best as they had done in the late 1980s when the car was devised.

Strangely, it was on the racetrack, a role for which some claim the car was never intended, that it finally found its vocation, dominating the 1995 global sportscar championship, including the gruelling Le Mans, to such an extent that you began to wonder why the others cars bothered turning up at all.

If it looks like gold lining the engine bay, that's because it is. Gold is the best heat reflector a lot of money can buy. The BMW-built, 6.1-litre, V12 engine is a masterpiece and, fitted to a McLaren, also terrifying to the uninitiated.

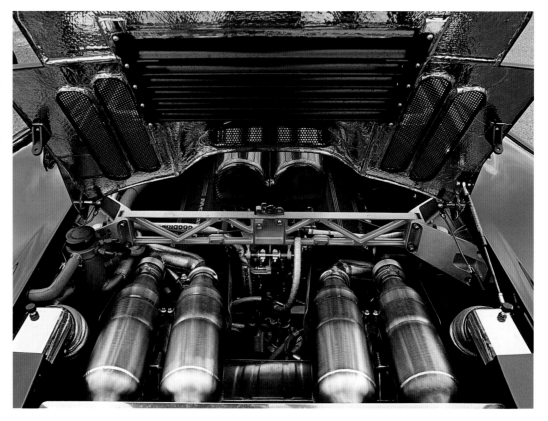

Opposite: Each FI comes complete with a plaque detailing all of McLaren's greatest motor-racing achievements. It can be updated when the car is in for servicing.

McLaren F1

Manufactured: 1993-97
Number of cars: c100

Dimensions
Length: 4,288mm
Width: 1,820mm
Height: 1,140mm
Wheelbase: 2,718mm
Front track/rear track: 1,568mm/1,472mm
Kerb weight: 1,138kg

Engine
Capacity: 6,064cc
Bore/stroke: 86mm/87mm
Construction: Aluminium head,
   aluminium block
Valve gear: 4 valves per cylinder, dohc
Compression ratio: 10.5:1
Max power: 627bhp at 7,400rpm
Max torque: 479lb ft at 4,000rpm
Gearbox: 6-speed manual

Brakes
Front: Ventilated discs
Rear: Ventilated discs
Servo assistance/anti-lock: No/no

Suspension
Front: Double wishbones, coil springs,
   anti-roll bar
Rear: Double wishbones, coil springs,
   anti-roll bar

Steering system
Unassisted rack and pinion

Wheels and tyres
Wheel size: 9.0 x 17in (f), 11.5 x 17in (r)
Construction: Alloy
Tyre size: 235/45 ZR 17 (f), 315/45 ZR 17 (r)

Claimed performance
0-97kph (0-60mph): 3.2sec
Max speed: 381kph (237mph)

The men behind the
McLaren – from left to
right: Gordon Murray,
the designer, Ron Dennis,
boss of McLaren Cars,
and Paul Rosche, head of
BMW Motorsports.

A novel three-seater
cabin has a central driving
position. Seat locations
are not ideal for face-to-
face conversations.

The F1 has no shortage of great names to its credit. It was designed by Gordon Murray, the creator of Formula One World-Championship-winning Brabhams and McLarens, and developed by Dr Jonathan Palmer, not simply a successful F1 driver but also one of the best test drivers in the business. It was styled by Peter Stevens, whose other credits include the revised Lotus Esprit, the second-generation Lotus Elan and the Jaguar XJR-15.

Those who own F1s tend to keep quiet about it, liking its relative lack of visual ostentation. The Sultan of Brunei, however, is believed to own five while the wealthy German banker, Dr Thomas Bscher, has two, one for the road, one for the track.

Perhaps the most remarkable stories of the F1 come from those who have crashed them. Bernd Pischetsreider, chairman of BMW, managed to turn one over without harming any of the occupants, but that is nothing compared with the accident involving the first ever prototype. During hot-weather testing in the Namibian desert, the test driver lost control at over 273kph (170mph). The car somersaulted, nose over tail, deep into the desert. When it finally came to rest, the driver simply popped open the door, unclipped his safety belt and walked away from the wreck without so much as a scratch.

No one has yet discovered exactly how fast an F1 will go. During high-speed tests at the Nardo test track in Italy, Jonathan Palmer managed to drive the third proto-type around the banked track at an average lap speed of 372kph (231mph). Given that, at such a velocity on a banked surface, much of your speed is lost in tyre scrub, it would certainly have gone considerably faster on the flat ... especially since its early engine was, at the very least, 50bhp down on the production version.

The McLaren road car was a financial failure but it soon earned a healthy living as a racer, winning the Le Mans 24-hour race at its first attempt in 1995. The Harrods-backed car led for 21-hours, driven by Derek and Justin Bell, but it fell back to third after the gearbox started to fail.

Ferrari Dino 246GT

The 246GT is the car that proved a mid-engined layout could be made to work and be forgiving in a road car.

If you see a Ferrari badge on a Dino 246GT, it is because its owner put it there. None, in fact, left the factory wearing anything other than the signature of Enzo Ferrari's late son. To conclude, however, that this made the 246 anything less than a proper Ferrari would indeed be a grave mistake.

For sure, the Dino was the least powerful road car ever to be created by Ferrari, starting life as the 180bhp 206GT before its 2-litre engine was stretched to 2.4-litres for the 246 version. But if ever there was a car that proved there is more to the magic of Maranello than pure speed, the little Dino was emphatically it.

For a start, there are its looks, one of Pininfarina's landmark shapes, curvaceous without seeming contrived, masking its considerable length to perfection and utterly delectable when viewed from almost every angle. Inside it was better still. You can see the two front wings rising up either side of the windscreen and the beautiful instruments crammed into a central binnacle behind the three-spoked, leather-rimmed, alloy steering wheel.

The driving position is pure Ferrari, all arms and no legs, while the gearbox, with its exposed, chromed gate and first on the bottom-left dog-leg, is perhaps the marque's most famous calling card.

The engine does not catch at first. The six carburettor chokes need priming precisely before the little V6 engine will spin into life. But when it does, you will know that few cars in the world have ever been fitted with a motor of this calibre. Even when the engine is at idle, its sound is so full, so rich and packed with promise of what is to follow that you scarcely dare look at the rev counter to see how long the joy will last. The red sector starts at 7,750rpm, a height approached by no other manufacturer back in the mid-seventies.

On the road, its behaviour was not like that of any Ferrari that had come before or was to follow; it was much better. Its handling, for example, finally laid to rest the myth that a mid-engine layout inevitably led to tricky on-limit handling. The Dino's limits were not simply beyond the reach of almost everything on the road in its day, but when the limit did arrive, it did so with such well-lit warnings from the chassis and steering that you would need to be unusually unlucky or insensitive to chance upon it unwittingly. And even if you did, the

Dino would still, by and large, look out for you in a way that its successors – the 308, 328 and 348 – would not recognize.

Most of all though, the Dino was one of those happy cars where all the elements of driving enjoyment gelled together as one. It wasn't hugely quick, although its top speed of 240kph (149mph), while routine today, was pretty impressive a generation ago. But that didn't seem to matter. What mattered more was that the Dino not only looked right, it sounded right and felt right, too.

Ferrari's history is a story of predominately great cars creating a legend against which its mistakes, few in number yet significant nonetheless, can lean for support. There is a certain presumption that if a car wears a Ferrari badge, it must be brilliant, and those who take this view will only occasionally be disappointed.

The Dino wore no Ferrari badges nor could it rely on a smokescreen of speed to blank out its shortcomings. It had to survive and earn its place in the history of the world's greatest sporting marque on talent alone. It succeeded to take its place not

Overleaf: A beautiful profile of a very cleverly designed car. Pininfarina styled it so that it looked like a baby Ferrari, although if you bothered to measure it, it was actually rather large.

This, a later 1974-model Dino, can be identified by the flared wheelarches. It was replaced by the ugly and unloved 308GT4 the next year.

Ferrari Dino 246GT

Manufactured: 1969-74
Number of cars: 3,761

Dimensions
Length: 4,234mm
Width: 1,707mm
Height: 1,143mm
Wheelbase: 2,344mm
Front track/rear track: n/a
Kerb weight: 1,081kg

Engine
Capacity: 2,418cc
Bore/stroke: 93mm/60mm
Construction: Aluminium head,
 cast-iron block
Valve gear: 2 valves per cylinder, dohc
Compression ratio: 9.0:1
Max power: 195bhp at 7,600rpm
Max torque: 166lb ft at 5,500rpm
Gearbox: 5-speed manual

Brakes
Front: Ventilated discs
Rear: Ventilated discs
Servo assistance/anti-lock: Yes/no

Suspension
Front: Double wishbones, coil springs,
 anti-roll bar
Rear: Double wishbones, coil springs,
 anti-roll bar

Steering system
Unassisted rack and pinion

Wheels and tyres
Wheel size: 6.5 x 14in
Construction: Alloy
Tyre size: 205/70 VR 14

Claimed performance
0-97kph (0-60mph): 6.8sec
Max speed: 241kph (150mph)

The rear of a Dino is just as pretty as the front. You can see how little body protection was offered by the bumpers, but not by the almost total absence of rust proofing. Like almost all Italian cars of the era, Dinos turned to dust if not looked after.

Luggage room was provided behind the engine with space only for the spare wheel in the nose.

among the five finest road cars the factory ever produced.

Even among Ferraris, the Dino had a dazzling silver-screen career. Tony Curtis starred in *The Persuaders* as Danny Wilde, a self-made millionaire foiling Roger Moore's Lord Brett Sinclair almost as well as his extremely early Dino was a match for Moore's Aston Martin DB5. Hollywood's fascination with the Dino did not stop there, either – one starring in the first (and better) of the two *Cannonball Run* movies, a second propelling another preposterously wealthy amateur sleuth in his fight against evil. This time it was Robert Wagner driving across the screen in the opening credits of that definitive American detective drama of the 1980s, *Hart to Hart*, with Stephanie Powers playing both wife and Mercedes-Benz SL driver.

A less well known but perhaps rather more compelling appearance was in the seventies' thriller, *Eleven, Harrowhouse*, where Candice Bergen, starring with Charles Grodin, James Mason and Trevor Howard, plays not only a suicidally quick driver but also a co-conspirator in the largest diamond robbery ever attempted in London. This time, the Dino's co-stars were two more British stalwarts – a Jaguar MkII and a Lotus Europa.

In reality, thanks to its irresistible charms, the Dino has found itself in the hands of many more world-famous stars. Prince Michael of Kent used to have one while George Harrison's famous yellow example was only recently sold at auction. It is a car that designers love, too, which is why Julian Thompson, head of car design at Lotus, has an example tucked away.

The legendary late jazz musician Ronnie Scott was an owner as is television and radio bad boy Chris Evans, while Noel Edmonds, another incurable car enthusiast, used to drive a 246 bedecked from stem to stern in the livery of Olympus cameras.

Do not be fooled by the Ferrari badge on this and other Dinos. No 246 ever left the factory bearing one, since the Dino was intended to be looked on as a marque in its own right. Finding a Dino today without such a badge, however, is not easy.

Jaguar E-type 3.8

A convertible E-type was launched at the same time as the coupé. It looked almost as good, too, and has always commanded a higher price.

Say the name 'E-type' anywhere in the civilized world and if the response is one of less than warm enthusiasm it is safe to say you have stumbled across either another band of tiresome car haters or aliens on a day trip from another planet. The E-type is the sportscar exemplified and has been that way since 1961.

At the time, nobody could quite believe it. The man behind the masterpiece was William Lyons and the lines he created will be remembered for all time as one of the defining shapes in the evolution of the sportscar. In the endless bonnet, with its slats and bulges, lay the promise of untold power, while the sleekness of its profile, the fared-in headlamps and perfectly proportioned coupé cabin told the story of a car shaped by the wind. Those who were there

found it impossible to imagine how a car could ever look more modern or rakish.

It meant business, too. Under that enormous bonnet lay a 3.8-litre version of the straight-six engine that brought about five victories at Le Mans, producing an alleged 265bhp and a top speed of 240kph (150mph) while its nearest rival, the Aston Martin DB4, cost about twice the price and struggled to do 225kph (140mph). The cabin was a masterpiece of style and function. Ahead sat the two main dials with beautiful white-on-black faces, while the centre console was an orderly spread of minor instruments and ancillary switches. Best of all was the steering wheel, which was a classic wood-rimmed affair with drilled alloy spokes and a Jaguar leaping out of the boss at you.

In its day, the four-speed Moss gearbox attracted some criticism for being slow and interrupting the flow of power from the engine. Today, however, its solid, heavy feel seems entirely appropriate, while the crisp bark of the legendary twin-cam motor as the rev counter needle sails around the dial is soaked in the memories of the 1960s.

By modern standards it is still quick, but not exceptionally so. A BMW 328i saloon, for example, would quickly disappear into the distance – but speed is not now the E-type's charm. While once the E-type was revered as being the most forward-thinking car of its time, now it is its values as a classic car that make it so hugely popular. Its abilities, once at the cutting edge, now do no more than provide the route through its charms, which, like most of the best classics, revolve rather less around what they will do than the manner in which they do it.

It is, in fact, the ultimate classic for pragmatists – gorgeous enough that a lifetime's familiarity will not dull its appeal yet fast enough that it will not bore even the most demanding of drivers.

Historians will adore it for the heritage under its bonnet and the fact that its design came from the XKSS, the glorious road-going version of the D-type racer whose life was ended by a factory fire after just 17 examples had been built. Aesthetes will love not simply its style but also the quality of its complex construction, while the practically minded among them will find attraction in the dependability of those cars that have been properly maintained. The fact that today's new XK8 does so much to ape its style and values speaks volumes: in the car world as much as in that of humans, imitation remains the most sincere form of flattery.

Overleaf: It was only the earliest, Series One E-types that retained all the grace of the original design. Through the years the E-type became longer, taller and fatter, making it, by the 1970s, a sad parody of its former beauty.

Its shape is the work of the brilliant Malcolm Sayer, who also designed the C- and D-type racers. Its elegant profile is one of the most distinctive shapes created in the 1960s. Good air-flow helped to give credibility to its top speed claims.

One of the most famous views in automotive history –
the E-type bonnet has become legendary. The dashboard
layout – too often imitated and rarely bettered – is
close to perfection.

The E-type didn't need famous owners,
although it had hundreds of them – from
those who raced them in the early 1960s to
those, like world land- and water-speed
record breaker Donald Campbell, who had
them simply because nothing else suited
their lifestyles as well. The truth was, the E-
type was more famous in its own right than
any of its owners. Along with the Mini and
the mini-skirt it became a fashion icon in
the decade where fashion mattered more
than anything else.

It also found fame on celluloid, its curv-
ing shape and promise of power making it
a natural film star. It made a brilliant baddies' car, never better when painted black
and trying to mow down John Wayne in
his penultimate film, *Brannigan*.

Jaguar E-type 3.8

Manufactured: 1961-65
Number of cars: 15,490

Dimensions

Length: 4,455mm
Width: 1,657mm
Height: 1,220mm
Wheelbase: 2,430mm
Front track/rear track: 1270mm/1270mm
Kerb weight: 1,250kg

Engine

Capacity: 3,781cc
Bore/stroke: 87mm/106mm
Construction: Aluminium head, cast-iron block
Valve gear: 2 valves per cylinder, dohc
Compression ratio: 8.0:1
Max power: 265bhp at 5,500rpm
Max torque: 260lb ft at 4,000rpm
Gearbox: 4-speed manual

Brakes

Front: Plain discs
Rear: Plain discs
Servo assistance/anti-lock: Yes/no

Suspension

Front: Double wishbones, torsion bars,
    anti-roll bar
Rear: Lower wishbones, torsion bars, radius
    arms, anti-roll bar

Steering system

Unassisted rack and pinion

Wheels and tyres

Wheel size: 5.0 x 15in
Construction: Steel, spoked
Tyre size: 6.5 x 15in crossplies

Claimed performance

0-97kph (0-60mph): 6.9sec
Max speed: 241kph (150mph) plus

Opposite (both): The E-type cabin works thanks to sensible ergonomics. Very British instruments and an alloy-spoked, wood-rimmed wheel provide all the right 1960s' cues, too, and the engine is started with a button.

This, one of the most enduring engines of all time, first saw the light of day in 1948 when it was created for the XK120. It went on to power cars to five Le Mans victories before taking up residence in the E-type. Production continued well into the 1980s in the Jaguar XJ6 saloon and Daimler limousines and hearses.

The gill-like slats in the bonnet were required not simply to keep the engine cool but also to suck enough air into the three huge SU carburettors.

Long, thin rear lights not only perpetuated the overall styling theme of the car, but they also kept out of the way of the air-flow over its body.

Most, however, will recall in sickeningly accurate detail the destruction of two on an Italian mountain road in *The Italian Job*. During the sequence, Michael Caine has to watch helplessly as a bulldozer smashes to bits both an E-type coupé and convertible before his own Aston Martin DB4 is tipped over the side of the mountain.

The tragedy of the E-type story, however, was the perversion of its design over the years until it died, a fat, bloated travesty of the car it had once been. By the end it was longer, more bulbous, had rear seats, power steering and the option of an automatic gearbox. Its sole saving grace was an all new 5.3-litre V12 engine that had been commissioned not to create any kind of super E-type but merely to restore its original performance, which it just about managed to do. When the end came, not a moment too soon in 1974, just the engine survived to blossom into another Jaguar great and, like the straight six before it, become a multiple Le Mans winner.

A huge bulge in the nose was created partly for show, partly because it was needed. The view down the bonnet is one of the most evocative in all motoring.

Alfa-Romeo 8C

In the early 1930s, Grand Prix cars were not as they are today. They had two seats, competed on road as well as the track and were often developed directly from rather more humdrum, exclusively road-going vehicles. And thanks to this design flexibility, most of those that have survived the passing years are used less frequently for their original purpose of outright racing and more for their designed-in abilities on the public road.

And the most beautiful, as well as the best, of all such cars was the Alfa-Romeo 8C 2300 Monza. As a racing car, its successes became every bit as much the stuff of legend as those who drove them. The Monza name came from its victory in the 1931 Italian Grand Prix driven by Campari and Nuvolari, the latter also winning the

1932 Monaco Grand Prix and the first two of its three consecutive Targa Florio victories from 1931-33. Rudi Carraciola stole the 1932 Eifelrennen in one while Varzi carried off the 1934 Mille Miglia and Tim Birkin claimed the 1931 Le Mans 24-hour race. It entered the finest races of its day and, sooner or later, won them all.

You might not think a 1930s' Grand Prix car would translate well on to the public roads of the late 20th century, but you'd be wrong. Thanks to the extraordinary abilities of the straight-eight engine designed for it by the great Vittorio Jano, an 8C is as flexible and forgiving today as it was fast and furious then.

Despite its classic looks, it is that engine, with its ground-breaking design, that is the 8C's most stunning component. It was known at the time that a large number of cylinders and supercharging was the best way to extract large amounts of power from an engine, but mounting all eight cylinders in a line made it difficult to keep components that needed both to turn and run the length of the engine, such as the crankshaft and camshafts, from tearing themselves to pieces. Jano's solution, therefore, was in effect to design two short, stable, four-cylinder engines and join them together, extracting the power from both units at the point of their union, not at one end. The result was an engine that could rev higher for longer, produce more power and stay reliable not simply over a Grand Prix distance but for many thousands of miles.

Today, the 8C is one of those rare marvels, hardly ever seen in anything other than full flight, engine roaring its extraordinary song, supercharger whining at full effort. While just ten were originally built, a further 16 were constructed after 1933 by Enzo Ferrari's racing team, while the subsequent conversion of period Alfa-Romeo saloons into lovingly respectful replicas means that many more exist today that in their heyday.

Their popularity stems not simply from their looks and performance, even though a

Overleaf: A small cabin means that long distances are not ideal. For short blasts, however, the 8C takes some beating.

An 8C is stark, although with headlights fitted it is entirely road legal. It was more than capable of driving to the racetrack, winning the race and driving straight home again.

Alfa-Romeo 8C

Manufactured: 1931
Number of cars: 10

Dimensions
Length: n/a
Width: n/a
Height: 1,200mm
Wheelbase: 2,650mm
Front track/rear track: 1,380mm/1,380mm
Kerb weight: 1,250kg

Engine
Capacity: 2,336cc
Bore/stroke: 65mm/88mm
Construction: Aluminium head,
   aluminium block
Valve gear: 2 valves per cylinder, dohc
Compression ratio: 6.5:1
Max power: 178bhp at 5,400rpm
Max torque: n/a
Gearbox: 4-speed manual

Brakes
Front: Drums
Rear: Drums
Servo assistance/anti-lock: No/no

Suspension
Front: Rigid axle, semi-elliptic
   longitudinal springs
Rear: Rigid axle, semi-elliptic
   longitudinal springs

Steering system
Unassisted worm and sector

Wheels and tyres
Wheel size: 6.0 x 19in
Construction: Steel, spoked
Tyre size: 5.5 x 19in crossplies

Claimed performance
0-97kph (0-60mph): 8sec (estimated)
Max speed: 209kph (130mph) (estimated)

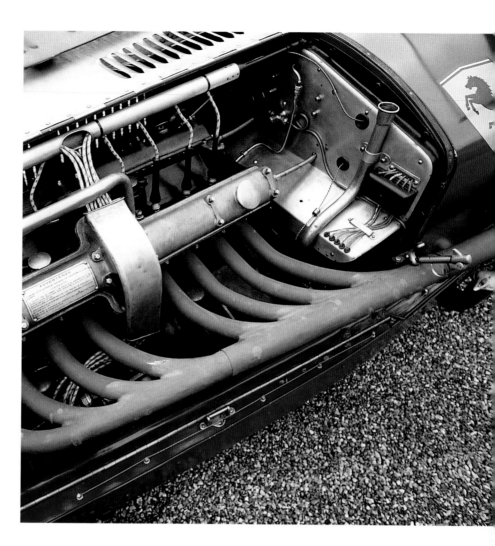

Vittorio Jano was responsible for the mighty straight-eight engine, which was, in fact, two separate four-cylinder engines sharing a common crankshaft. Power was taken from the middle of the engine and sent to the rear wheels via a four-speed gearbox without synchromesh. Once you hear its noise, you will never forget it.

Opposite: The cockpit is dominated by a giant steering wheel needed to keep helm efforts low, and almost as big a rev-counter. This is by far the most important dial when you are racing – a speedometer is surplus to requirements. The spindly gear lever is a little difficult to move around the gate for those not used to pre-war gear boxes, but it gets easier with practice.

top speed of 209kph (130mph) for a car of its age is nearly unprecedented. More than anything, the 8C is just wonderful to drive, from its fine brakes to handling that would genuinely stun all those who think cars of that era need not do much more than look at a corner before falling over.

Many compete in latter-day re-creations of the Mille Miglia, and those who follow along in modern road cars find, to their astonishment that, unless they are in something with at least the performance of a Porsche, they are simply unable to keep up. Today such performance is extra-ordinary, in 1931 it must have been just about beyond belief.

8C Alfa-Romeos raced for Scuderia Ferrari, hence the famous prancing horse emblem on its flank.

The most famous exponent of the 8C today must be Alain de Cadenet. He has two, one of which he has used on occasions as an everyday car. He has entered it in gruelling events all over the world and raced it with success. It also used to be spotted, usually covered in the detritus that comes from hard days on the road, parked outside one of his favourite nightclubs.

Recently an Alfa-Romeo 8C was also added to Nick Mason's rare and fabulous collection of vehicles. Given that Mason's reputation for using his cars for the purpose for which they were designed is just about unsurpassed, it is to be presumed that it will not be long before this famous early team car is also seen out on the public roads once more.

The greatest stories of the 8C are, sadly, just that. The tale of Nuvolari following Varzi at night on the 1,600-km (1,000-mile) Mille Miglia road race has remained gloriously unrestrained by the limitations of mere truth. The legend says that Nuvolari, in an effort to get past his old rival, turned his headlamps off as the two charged at speed over the mountains. Varzi, believing Nuvolari to have crashed or retired, slowed his car to a more comfortable pace and was no wiser to the reality of the situation until he heard a roar as the 8C swept by, lights back on, in a blaze of triumph.

One story that, however, is undoubtedly true is that Sir Henry Birkin, unable to find a British-made car to suit his talents, entered the 1931 Le Mans 24-hour race with Lord Howe, which they duly won. Birkin was less than pleased to receive a telegram from Mussolini congratulating him on his 'win for Italy'.

These classic lines contain real and effortless beauty. The 8C was designed simply to be as fast as possible – meaning that these exquisite lines and near perfect proportions effectively happened on their own.

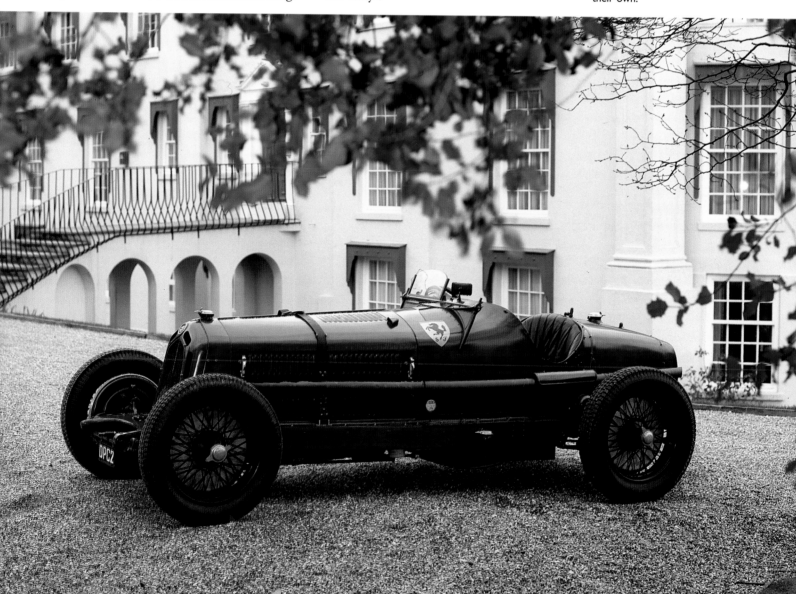

Rolls-Royce Silver Ghost

Many Rolls-Royces are called 'Silver Ghost' but all are, in fact, named in honour of a single car: the Silver Ghost, registration number AX201.

The Silver Ghost was a publicity stunt. Had it not been singled out, plated in silver and sent off on the most gruelling reliability run in existence at the time, it would have been no more or less than the twelfth Rolls-Royce 40/50hp down the line. In the event it became the most famous car in the world.

It is difficult to keep your mouth shut as you approach the Ghost. Its presence is mighty, larger even than its legend, while the detail of its form is the most exquisite you will find on any car. The lights, instruments, levers and ancillary fittings are all gems worthy of the highest praise.

You have to climb up to the driver's seat and while you sit there, someone who knows the car rather better, starts it up.

First, unchock the clutch from its bed in a pool of oil, then turn on the fuel tap and raise 2psi of pressure on the hand pump. Then open the bonnet and press down on the carburettor float until it floods, enrich the mixture by turning a lever on the dashboard and fully retard the ignition by tugging back another lever. Set the hand throttle, walk to the front of the car, unhook the starting handle and turn it eight times to suck up the freshly prepared mixture. Return to the cockpit, switch on the magneto, flick the trembler coils, walk back to the starting handle, turn once and, invariably, the 7-litre engine will start.

And if this sounds tricky, it's nothing compared with driving it. The principal problems are that you need to change gear by the time the engine has hit 1,200rpm (barely above modern idling speed), but there is no rev-counter. The gearbox has neither spring loading nor synchromesh, so each change takes two dips of the clutch and faultless matching of engine and transmission speed. As well, the footbrake does not work above walking pace, leaving the hand brake and the back of the car in front as your two options for stopping.

You would think it would be a nightmare to drive. It is, in fact, a joy. What you have to remember is that this is a Rolls-Royce,

and until you relax you stand no chance of progressing with anything less than complete amateurism. Take your time, slur your changes together and your progress soon takes on a majestic quality. The engine's note is beautifully deep and musical and you do not even need to worry about the brakes: it's inconceivable that someone will fail to see you coming.

Back in 1907, the sight of the Ghost would have had considerably greater impact than that of a McLaren F1 today. It was the Ghost that proved the potential

Overleaf: Despite its great value, the Ghost has never been a museum piece and works hard to this day.

The Ghost is stunning to look at in the flesh. Effortlessly beautiful, it set the tone for the marque that it still retains.

The 7-litre Ghost engine represents 1907 state-of-the-art motoring.

Rolls-Royce Silver Ghost

Manufactured: 1907
Number of cars: 1

Dimensions
Length: 4,572mm
Width: 914mm
Height: n/a
Wheelbase: 2,963mm
Front track/rear track: n/a
Chassis weight: 940kg

Engine
Capacity: 7,046cc
Bore/stroke: 114mm/114mm
Construction: Cast-iron head, cast-iron block
Valve gear: 2 valves per cylinder, side valve
    actuation
Compression ratio: 3.2:1
Max power: n/a
Max torque: n/a
Gearbox: 4-speed manual

Brakes
Front: None
Rear: Hand brake-operated drums
Servo assistance/anti-lock: No/no

Suspension
Front: Dead forged axle, 10 leaf springs, no
    shock absorbers
Rear: Fully floating axle, 13 longitudinal leaf
    springs and 11 transverse

Steering system
Unassisted, direct

Wheels and tyres
Wheel size: n/a
Construction: Wooden, spoked, ball bearing hubs
Tyre size: 875 x 105mm (f), 880 x 120mm (r)

Claimed performance
0-97kph (0-60mph): n/a
Max speed: 80kph (50mph)

long-term reliability of the car at a time when most drivers counted their blessings if a single journey was completed without breaking down. More importantly, it single handedly established the reputation of the most noble motoring marque of all.

The Silver Ghost has had an extremely active life, having covered close to 700,000 miles in the last 90 years. Sold originally by Rolls-Royce in 1908 to a man who owned a taxi company, it was bought back on his death in 1948 and has since worked around the world as a roving ambassador for the marque.

Its original fame came from the series of reliability tests it undertook when new. Most famous was the run from London to Edinburgh in 1907, completed entirely in

The Ghost's interior is comfortable, which must have been a blessing to all those who travelled non-stop from London to Scotland in it.

One of the most famous and instantly recognized profiles in the world.

top gear as part of a 12-day reliability trial. It came through unscathed. Rather more impressive was its attempt on the world reliability record, which stood at 11,408km (7,089 miles). By driving non-stop from London to Glasgow and back for seven weeks, the record was shattered, the car eventually stopping at 24,140km (15,000 miles). Given the state of the roads then, mostly unmade tracks, it would be no small feat to replicate today.

The Silver Ghost was the idea of neither Charles Rolls nor Henry Royce. Rolls was the salesman, Royce the engineer, but it was Claude Johnson, the business brain of the partnership, who dreamed up the name and bolted it to the bulkhead of the car, where it remains to this day.

The car that put Rolls-Royce on the road to being 'the best car in the world'.

Lamborghini Miura SV

The SV version of the Miura was the ultimate of the production variants and, some would argue, the first time the Miura could actually claim to be a truly good car.

It is a strange irony that, were it not for Ferrari, Lamborghini would never have been created. Thanks almost entirely to the on-going excellence of the Ferrari marque, Lamborghini has spent its entire existence battling for the credibility and prestige, as well as the sales-earning potential, that came to Ferrari from the start.

In 1966, though, that all seemed likely to change. That was the year Lamborghini unveiled the Miura and shocked the sportscar-loving world into a bigger silence even than that which followed the unveiling of the Jaguar E-type in 1961. For a start, the Miura was so beautiful that three of the world's greatest designers, Nuccio Bertone, Marcello Gandini and Giorgetto Giugiaro, all claimed it to be their work, sparking off

an argument that, rather more than three decades later, seems to be showing little sign of abating.

And if that was not enough to strike fear into the heart of Ferrari, the mechanical specification certainly did the trick. It was not that the 3.9-litre V12 was any greater or more powerful than the 4.4-litre unit Ferrari had up its sleeve, waiting to be installed in the 365GTB/4 'Daytona', it was rather the location of the engine that dug furrows in the brows at Maranello. It was slung across the back of the car, behind the driver, to create a mid-engined, transversely mounted twelve-cylinder configuration, which, to this day, has never been repeated.

Mercifully for Ferrari, the original Miura was nothing like as good as it looked or sounded. Though quick, it was soon clear that it was not quite as fast as had been suggested, which, given that the car was not simply heavy but also tricky to handle, was perhaps no bad thing.

It was not until 1970 and the release of the ultimate Miura, the SV, that, at last, Lamborghini provided the waiting world with a truly convincing answer to the Daytona. Differentiated from previous Miuras by the deletion of the distinctive eyelashes around the headlights, it at last went every bit as fast as it looked.

No wonder. In its final, SV-iteration, the 3,929cc, quad-cam V12 engine had been coaxed into providing 385bhp, way up at 7,850rpm. It provided a sizeable problem for the rival Ferrari, which not only still had its engine old-fashionedly under the bonnet but also produced a mere 352bhp.

Over the years some have questioned the true output of the SV, while others have suggested that, side by side, the heavier and allegedly less powerful Daytona was, in fact, at least as swift, if not faster. In truth, none of this really mattered. What was important was that, in the SV, Lamborghini at last had a car to tackle Ferrari head on.

Today, the Miura continues to stand out as a seriously flawed car, one whose faults need to be adapted to and driven around before true driving pleasure can be found. But if you can conquer the awful driving position and cluttered cabin and come to terms with a chassis that, while improved, had still yet to discover truly how to conquer the inherent on-limit aggression of the mid-engined layout, there is an escapist's dream waiting.

To listen to the rise and fall of the wondrous V12, hearing each gear snap into place as you work the gear lever through its exposed gate, and know from the faces of all you pass that there remains still just a handful of road-going shapes with even half the visual impact of the SV, is to enjoy an irreplaceable motoring experience.

The Miura was followed by the quicker but rather overrated Countach. It would be a generation before Lamborghini once more produced another with its spirit. It was a Diablo and it, too, wears SV badges.

Overleaf: Who styled this car? Marcello Gandini, Giorgetto Giugiaro and the late Nuccio Bertone have all, at some time, claimed it as their own.

A wide, low rear stance hid the transverse V12 engine, the first, and last, to be so installed in the world. Power is fine, noise close to incredible.

The cabin is more suited to primates than humans thanks to a ridiculously long-arm, short-leg driving position. Instrumentation, in the finest tradition of the Italian supercar was not exactly ideal either.

No wonder Miuras had a reputation for somewhat tricky handling when you take into account the size, power and location of the engine and then consider those skinny little tyres through which it was all meant to reach the ground.

Lamborghini Miura SV

Manufactured: 1971-72
Number of cars: 150

Dimensions
Length: 4,390mm
Width: 1,780mm
Height: 1,100mm
Wheelbase: 2,504mm
Front track/rear track: 1,412mm/1,541mm
Kerb weight: 1,245kg

Engine
Capacity: 3,929cc
Bore/stroke: 82mm/62mm
Construction: Aluminium head,
  aluminium block
Valve gear: 2 valves per cylinder, dohc
Compression ratio: 10.7:1
Max power: 385bhp at 7,850rpm
Max torque: 294lb ft at 5,750rpm
Gearbox: 5-speed manual

Brakes
Front: Ventilated discs
Rear: Ventilated discs
Servo assistance/anti-lock: Yes/no

Suspension
Front: Double wishbones, coil springs,
  anti-roll bar
Rear: Double wishbones, coil springs,
  anti-roll bar

Steering system
Unassisted rack and pinion

Wheels and tyres
Wheel size: 7.0 x 15in (f), 9.0 x 15in (r)
Construction: Alloy
Tyre size: 215/70 VR 15 (f), 225/60 VR 15 (r)

Claimed performance
0-97kph (0-60mph): 6sec
Max speed: 289kph (180mph)

It is the best beginning of any car movie ever filmed. The camera pans across the Italian Alps to catch a bright orange Miura howling across the barren landscape. You can hear the rasp of the hard pressed V12 motor and see how bizarrely low and lithe its shape really is.

Inside an immaculately suave driver, cigarette in hand, sunglasses on, guides the Lamborghini around the perilous twists and turns and rockets flat out and disappears into a tunnel. Then, a brief squeal of brakes, a rifle-crack explosion and a ball of flame curling around the tunnel walls. The Miura has hit a bulldozer kindly placed at the tunnel exit by the Mafia . . . So starts *The Italian Job* and with it the Miura's finest claim to fame. So the story goes, the wreck that was pushed over the side of the mountain was indeed a Miura, albeit a Miura that had had its valuable engine carefully removed.

The Miura has attracted some likely and some not so likely owners over the years. You might not be too surprised to learn that Rod Stewart was an owner and appreciator of this most outlandish of road cars, and you might even expect the Aga Khan to have one in his impressive stable of motors. Few, however, would predict that Frank Sinatra was able to place himself among that exclusive band of people who, at some stage, have owned Miuras.

The Lamborghini emblem, left, depicts a raging bull, a theme carried through in the Miura badge, above. The company came into being when Ferruccio Lamborghini was so disappointed with his Ferrari that he thought he could do better himself.

A wonder when seen on the public road – some would say that the Miura is the most beautiful sportscar of all time. It is perhaps no wonder that so many claim themselves to be the author of those lines.

Lancia Stratos

The good news is that the Lancia Stratos is one car that is every bit as mad as it looks.

There is a common thread running through the road reports that were published about the Lancia Stratos during its heyday in the mid 1970s. Fear. While other supercars engendered love, respect or even contempt, fear was a closed shop with a Stratos badge on the door.

At first it is hard to see why. After all, its Ferrari Dino 246GT-derived engine produced under 200bhp, a figure easily bested by some family saloons today. It is only as you walk towards the Stratos that the butterflies start to flutter. The shape contrives to be both gorgeous and mad; not only does the distance between the front and rear wheels seem impossibly short, the wraparound windscreen seem to suggest the driver will need to spend at least as much time looking out of the side of the car as the front. Which is a worry.

Fall rather than climb in, and land in an impossibly bunched driving position with your feet roughly where you would ideally like your knees, and your arms as straight as drainpipes. There are instruments everywhere, seemingly sprayed at random around the dashboard. Look in the door and see a big capacious bin, like a question mark on its side. Some nodding gesture to practicality in this most alien of road car environments? No, its where you store your helmet.

Look at the body's construction. Nothing seems to fit. There are many more Stratos replicas in the world than the genuine article and those who know about such things will tell you that the best way to tell a proper Stratos from a fake is to look at the panel gaps. If it looks like its been properly built, it is one of the fakes.

Fear is now a real factor and the engine is not even running. Fire up the quad-cam, 2.4-litre motor. Apart from its exhaust, it is identical to that in the Dino but is claimed

to have just 190bhp, not the usual 195bhp. The story goes that, apparently, Enzo refused to allow a Lancia to be seen to have as much power as a Ferrari.

It actually moves along the road very sweetly. The engine is noisy because the Stratos carries no sound-deadening material but, with a note produced by a power plant related to that which took Mike Hawthorn to the Formula One World Championship in 1958, it is not a noise you would be without. It feels quick, but not scarily so. Using all 8,000rpm the engine permits, it bowls you along at about the same sort of rate as a rather more powerful but heavier Porsche 911 of today. Fear recedes.

It is a corner, so you turn in gently on a constant throttle. Pandemonium. The car is going straight on, the front tyres seemingly bereft of grip. So you snap the throttle shut and find the situation re-versed, with the nose now charging at the apex, the back flailing around and you wondering if you have enough time to unwind all that extra lock before it throws it, and you, through the hedge. You gather it all up, still in the first third of the corner and gently squeeze open the acceleration. Chaos returns. You realize why it needs that wraparound windscreen.

The Stratos was not designed for mere mortals. Its purpose in life was to win ral-lies, something it did with monotonous regularity. And on the special stages, agility is everything, which is why the Stratos is designed to change direction as fast as you can think, and to do so on commands from brake and accelerator as well as steering. Once mastered, however, it contains some kind of ultimate experience for those few talented enough to keep up with it. Every-body else would do well to stay away.

The utterly impractical Stratos shape was designed for agility not beauty, but somehow managed both.

Overleaf: The wraparound windscreen is needed by rally drivers who drove the Stratos sideways.

Lancia Stratos

Manufactured: 1972-75
Number of cars: 400

Dimensions
Length: 3,710mm
Width: 1,750mm
Height: 1,114mm
Wheelbase: 2,180mm
Front track/rear track: 1,430mm/1,460mm
Kerb weight: 980kg

Engine
Capacity: 2,418cc
Bore/stroke: 93mm/60mm
Construction: Aluminium head, cast-iron block
Valve gear: 2 valves per cylinder, dohc
Compression ratio: 9.0:1
Max power: 190bhp at 7,000rpm
Max torque: 168lb ft at 4,000rpm
Gearbox: 5-speed manual

Brakes
Front: Ventilated discs
Rear: Ventilated discs
Servo assistance/anti-lock: No/no

Suspension
Front: Double wishbones, coil springs,
    anti-roll bar
Rear: McPherson struts, coil springs,
    anti-roll bar

Steering system
Unassisted rack and pinion

Wheels and tyres
Wheel size: 6.5 x 14in
Construction: Alloy
Tyre size: 205/70 VR 14

Claimed performance
0-97kph (0-60mph): 6sec (estimated)
Max speed: 225kph (140mph) (estimated)

The Stratos engine came straight from a Ferrari Dino, but Enzo Ferrari forced Lancia to claim it had less power, since he didn't want a Lancia to be as powerful as a Ferrari. The V6 motor is strong if looked after well and it suits the Stratos. Though not hugely quick in its road-going form, the more highly developed racers, with nearer 300bhp, were apparently quite terrifying.

Opposite: Its interior is a joke; its driving position dismal; its instruments a mess; and switchgear haphazard to say the least. But this does not spoil the fun for a minute.

Cracked open like an egg, the Stratos's rudimentary simplicity is easy to see. Good access to components was vital on rally stages.

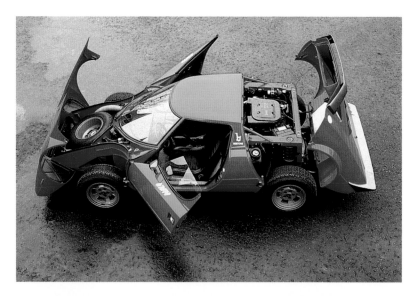

The Stratos's life began at the 1970 Turin Motor Show and – initially as a concept, then a rally car and finally a road car – kept in the headlines throughout the decade.

The names of those who brought the Stratos the distinction of becoming one of the most successful competition cars of all time read like a roll call of race and, in the main, rally greats. Developed by the late Ferrari ace Mike Parkes until his tragic death in a road-car accident in 1977, the Stratos competed in the world rally championship at first as an amusing diversion and, soon after, as the one unstoppable force in the field. Its drivers won the world rally championship outright three times in succession from 1974 to 1976, while the world's most famous events, such as the

Tail up and tearing up the highway.

102

Targa Florio and the Monte Carlo rally, were all conquered – the latter an incredible four times.

Driven by such rally heroes as Sandro Munari, Bjorn Waldegaard, Simo Lampinen and Marku Alen it was no stranger to racing drivers either, with Formula One stars, such as Arturo Merzario and Vittorio Brambilla, trying their luck with the vehicle. Its engine even found its way into a British Formula Two chassis, driven by Brambilla and another Formula One star of the future, Eddie Cheever. The car was entered by Ron Dennis in his days before

taking over as the boss of the incredibly successful McLaren Formula One team. Stratoses even competed at the punishing Le Mans – an event that could scarcely have been in the minds of those who designed it.

The Stratos's last win in a major rally championship came in 1979, after which the advent of the Audi Quattro, with its four wheel drive system, made all rally cars that had come before obsolete on the spot. Even so, it continued to find success in lesser events right up until 1982, a staggering ten years after its competition debut.

The Stratos looks altogether happier in its natural state. Lancia boasts the most successful rally record of them all and much of it was directly down to the Stratos's numerous wins.

Honda NSX

It was the big one, the car whose launch was heralded by the curious sound of the knees of Europe's supercar manufacturers knocking together as one. Japan had already had its first crack at such a car and the result, the Nissan 300ZX was pretty capable, but the Honda NSX promised to be something else again.

What was really worrying for the traditional supercar establishment was that the NSX seemed to cut no corners. While most of them were using steel for bodywork, the NSX came crafted from lighter, more durable aluminium. While they may have had four camshafts and four valves per cylinder, the NSX added variable valve timing and inlet manifolding. Far from being a cynical con whose weaknesses could be identified and exposed, it seemed to be very much the real thing.

It was. After just one week in an NSX you knew it to be the most fantastically

pragmatic supercar ever devised. For all its low-slung good looks and normally aspirated 3-litre engine pumping out a strong 274bhp, this was a supercar that was as happy in the centre of town as barrelling down an *autobahn* at 260kph (160mph). All the controls were light and all-round visibility excellent. It was a doddle to drive.

What, perhaps, was more surprising was that it was similarly easy to drive really fast. Many cars flatter to deceive at modest speeds, their inherent weaknesses only appearing when set tasks beyond the scope of everyday endeavour. Some had thought that if you took an NSX to a really tricky track and polished off 100 laps in both wet and dry conditions, it would undo itself.

In fact, all it undid was the reputations of most of the other cars on the circuit. You could thrash the engine up to its 8,000rpm red-line a thousand times in an afternoon, stand on the brakes from 225kph

(140mph) lap after lap, shriek sideways around corners and not once would you shake its composure. Apart from an unusual appetite for tyres, the only limitations it would reveal were those of the driver.

And even in this respect, the NSX was extraordinary. Right on the limit, at an effort exclusively reserved for the racetrack, the NSX would still be there, looking after your interests, giving ample warning not simply of how much grip remained in the tyres but also precisely what to expect if the mark was overstepped. Of its contemporaries, only the Lotus Esprit looked after its driver so unreasonably well.

Incredibly, at the time, some said this somehow made the NSX less of a car; because you didn't need to fight it, because it was on your side, it was emasculating to drive. Even if you do not dismiss this as utter nonsense, then it is certainly an extremely primitive way of looking at the most technologically advanced sportscar of its time. It was, however ill judged, a way of criticizing the car.

In the end, though, the NSX never did take over Europe. It was not that it lacked ability, for a time it was better than the equivalent cars from both Porsche and Ferrari, its relative lack of success stemmed in the main from an in-built reluctance to spend Ferrari-type money on a Honda.

Call it die-hard traditionalism, I prefer simple snobbery, but Honda learned the hard way, just as Nissan had and Mazda were about to, that at this level, in certain countries, simple ability coupled with fantastic looks count for very little compared with having the right type of badge attached to your nose.

Overleaf: The NSX tried hard to catch the magical flowing lines of classical Italian supercars, and very nearly pulled it off. The car is attractive but lacks that certain subtlety of line that distinguishes the best.

A removable roof panel became an option in 1995, when the car also gained power steering and the choice of automatic gears, complete with steering-mounted shift switches.

Honda NSX

Manufactured: 1990 (on-going)
Number of cars: 18,531 (to date)

Dimensions

Length: 4,425mm
Width: 1,810mm
Height: 1,170mm
Wheelbase: 2,530mm
Front track/rear track: 1,510mm/1,530mm
Kerb weight: 1,351kg

Engine

Capacity: 2,977cc
Bore/stroke: 90mm/78mm
Construction: Aluminium head,
    aluminium block
Valve gear: 4 valves per cylinder, dohc
Compression ratio: 10.2:1
Max power: 274bhp at 7,100rpm
Max torque: 210lb ft at 5,300rpm
Gearbox: 5-speed manual

Brakes

Front: Ventilated discs
Rear: Ventilated discs
Servo assistance/anti-lock: Yes/yes

Suspension

Front: Double wishbones, coil springs,
    anti-roll bar
Rear: Double wishbones, coil springs,
    anti-roll bar

Steering system

Power-assisted rack and pinion

Wheels and tyres

Wheel size: 7.0 x 16in (f), 8.5 x 17in (r)
Construction: Alloy
Tyre size: 215/50 ZR 16 (f), 245/40 ZR 17 (r)

Claimed performance

0-97kph (0-60mph): 5.3sec
Max speed: 254kph (158mph)

An NSX engine has a small capacity and does not use turbochargers but, thanks to Japanese engineering wizardry, is still able to generate 274bhp. A quad-cam, 24-valve motor has variable valve timing and split-length induction. It may not look like much but it sounds wonderful all the way from idle to its 8,000rpm red line and beyond. In town, it is uncannily smooth and docile, which makes the NSX as easy to drive as a Civic. Fuel consumption is remarkably good, too.

Opposite: The NSX's interior is a disappointment compared with the rest of the car. Although the driving position is fine, the entire look of the cabin does the car's image no favours at all.

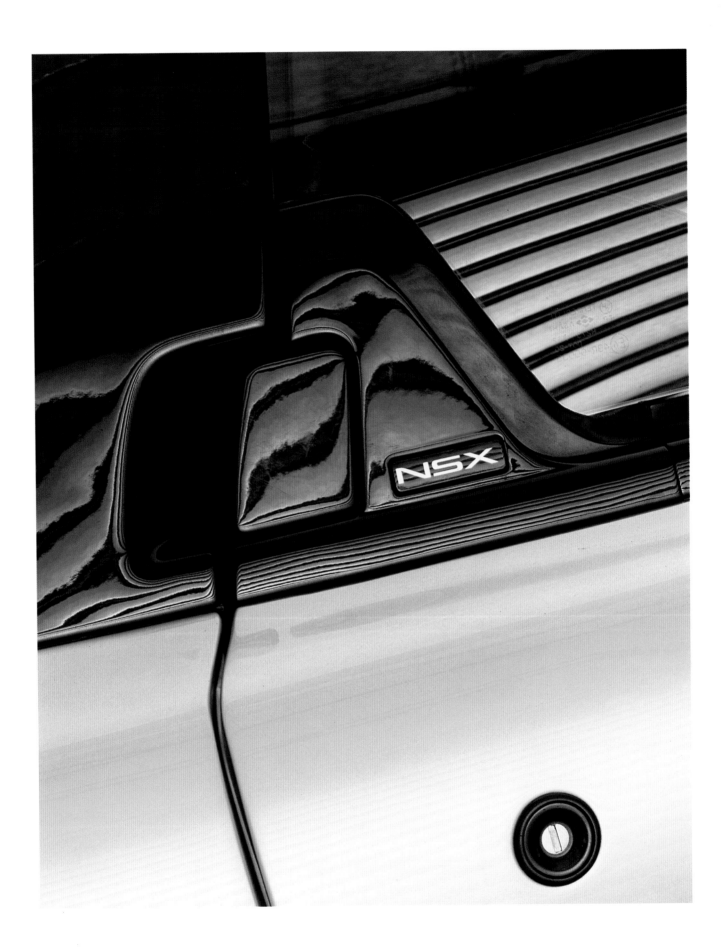

Ayrton Senna liked the NSX. He liked it a lot. He had dealerships that sold them in his native Brazil and also kept one as everyday transport while the Grand Prix circus kept him in Europe. He enjoyed the way they could be driven quietly and without ostentation in city traffic and he loved the way they would let him give full vent to his skills on the racetrack.

Around Silverstone in the most appalling weather conditions, he would slide the car sideways to the point where you knew it was just milliseconds from flying off the track. Then, at over 160kph (100mph), he would hold the car at 45 degrees to the intended direction of travel, one hand on the wheel, the other pointing to some bump that the NSX would cope with but might have thrown his Formula One McLaren offline. And all the time, he would be calmly commentating on what he was doing and politely enquiring whether, you strapped in beside him, were enjoying yourself.

Senna, in fact, was instrumental in the development of the NSX, which goes some way to explaining why its chassis capabilities had been developed so far beyond the point reached by its chief conceptual rivals from Mazda and Nissan. Senna drove early prototypes both in Japan and at Germany's Nürburgring, the most challenging and exciting race track in the world.

Gordon Murray, the South African who was McLaren's technical director during the Senna era as well as the designer of a wealth of ultra-successful Formula One racing cars, is another NSX devotee, subjecting his to four hard years before swapping it for a BMW.

The NSX's most famous silver-screen appearance to date was in the highly acclaimed Quentin Tarantino movie blockbuster, *Pulp Fiction* . Driven in the film by Harvey Keitel, the NSX screams up to Tarantino's house where a headless corpse is in need of disposal.

You can see here where the NSX styling goes wrong. The nose works well but the space from the back of the door to the rear wheel is too long, making the Honda look a trifle ungainly.

BMW M1

BMW's M1 set handling standards that shook the supercar world to its very foundations. Not only would it grip like a Boxer or Countach, it would, unlike its rivals, also behave in an entirely reasonable fashion if you overstepped the mark.

It seems odd to associate BMW with either a mid-engined supercar or a project that ended in considerable financial loss, but the M1 was both.

The brainchild of Jochen Neerspach, the head of BMW's motorsports division, the original design brief was for a racing car that could double as a road machine and that would be styled and built in Italy, since BMW's in-house resources would not be easily adapted to such a project.

Lamborghini was employed and, had it not been for its own difficult financial circumstances, would have ended up building the Giugiaro-designed car at its factory north of Modena. In the end, however, BMW pulled out of the deal, awarded the contract to Baur in Germany, who built the road and race cars, while BMW lost money on every single one of them. Germany has not put a mid-engined supercar into production since that time.

What all of this contrives to obscure, however, is that the M1 was, and is, an exceptional motor car and one that, with better timing, a less-troubled conception and a more realistic list price, could have seen series production for a decade or more and truly challenged Italy's claim to be the home of the supercar.

That said, the M1 is not a car that, like the Ferrari Boxer or Lamborghini Countach with which it was charged to compete, is likely to capture your heart on first acquaintance. The body is attractive but not outstanding – although, if you see one today, you can appreciate that indefinable element of timelessness that would not have been evident in its day. Compared with the jaw-slackening drama of the Countach or effortless beauty of the Boxer, it looked a little plain.

Moreover, while they boasted purpose-built, twelve-cylinder powerhouse motors,

the M1 came propelled by a six-cylinder engine based on that found in the 7-series executive saloon, albeit it with a twin-cam, 24-valve cylinder head bolted on top. And while its 277bhp was impressive for the 3.5-litre capacity, it looked a little sick against the Ferrari's claimed 340bhp and Lamborghini's 375bhp. Love was most definitely not at first sight.

It did come, though, to those few lucky and stalwart enough to own an M1 and discover its hidden but very real charms. They discovered a supercar that worked in practice, not merely in principle. The engine, despite its comparatively humdrum specification, was soon rightly identified as one of the greats, capable of howling, snarling heroics one moment and total, unassuming docility the next. Nor was it slow, qualifying for then top slot supercar status with a 0-97kph (0-60mph) time of less than 6sec and a top speed in excess of 257kph (160mph).

And while the Italians might do all this and more, what they lacked was the M1's dependability and thoroughly executed design. Here was a mid-engined supercar designed in the genre's seventies' heyday, with ventilation that worked, electrics that could be relied on and the kind of build quality the Italian marques could scarcely credit. It was as at ease in traffic as it was on the open road or racetrack and, therefore, provided an everyday appeal second only to that of the less exotic Porsche 911.

It is a shame that the M1 story was so short and perceived to be so sad. It lacked the badge, beauty and power of those it sought to emulate and, it would have seemed at the time, possessed only their price tag. The simple truth that these presumptions clouded was that the M1 may not have been a shooting star in the blazing constellation of supercars, but it was a damn fine car and one that could hardly have deserved its fate less.

Giorgetto Giugiaro was responsible for the styling of the M1 as well as the VW Golf, Lotus Esprit, De Lorean and Fiat Punto. The result was not his finest effort but the M1 was attractive and, importantly, very purposeful.

Overleaf: The brief for the design of the M1 road car was for a car with all the passion of the established Italian supercars but without their often temperamental manners.

The stark M1 cabin is typically Teutonic and smacks of an era when function took priority over style. That said, it is one of BMW's least effective driving environments with a notably displaced driving position and haphazard switchgear. Even so, the seats are rather good and at least the ventilation works well – something that cannot always be guaranteed with supercars of this era.

BMW M1

Manufactured: 1978-81
Number of cars: 454

Dimensions
Length: 4,360mm
Width: 1,824mm
Height: 1,140mm
Wheelbase: 2,560mm
Front track/rear track: 1,550mm/1,576mm
Kerb weight: 1,322kg

Engine
Capacity: 3,453cc
Bore/stroke: 93mm/84mm
Construction: Aluminium head,
    cast-iron block
Valve gear: 4 valves per cylinder, dohc
Compression ratio: 9.0:1
Max power: 277bhp at 6,500rpm
Max torque: 243lb ft at 5,000rpm
Gearbox: 5-speed manual

Brakes
Front: Ventilated discs
Rear: Ventilated discs
Servo assistance/anti-lock: Yes/no

Suspension
Front: McPherson struts, coil springs,
    anti-roll bar
Rear: McPherson struts, coil springs,
    anti-roll bar

Steering system
Unassisted rack and pinion

Wheels and tyres
Wheel size: 7.0 x 16in (f), 8.0 x 16in (r)
Construction: Alloy
Tyre size: 205/55 VR 16 (f), 225/50 VR 16 (r)

Claimed performance
0-97kph (0–60mph): 5.6sec
Max speed: 261kph (162mph)

Motorsport's straight-six engine was based on that of
BMW's road saloons but it came with a twin-camshaft,
24-valve cylinder head to put power up from around
204bhp to a rather more meaningful 277bhp. Its
installation remains unique, with no other manufacturer
locating an in-line six into a mid-engined format. In
truth, though, the engine was hardly stressed at all in
the M1. It was later tuned to provide 340bhp in the last
of the BMW M5s but it was actually designed to handle
approximately 1000bhp when twin-turbocharged for
sportscar racing. In fact, rule changes meant that the M1
was a failure as a racing car, and it was only when the
Procar championship, featuring only M1s, was invented
that it gained serious competition history.

The idea of having a dedicated race series for M1s with all the top Formula One drivers taking part as a warm up race to the Grand Prix proper must have seemed brilliant. It would refloat the M1 race project, which had been beached by regulation changes, and cover BMW in almost all the glory of a Formula One manufacturer at a tiny fraction of the price.

There were problems, however. The rules called for the drivers occupying the first five places on the Grand Prix grid to take up M1s against the remainder of the non-Formula One drivers in the field. At the first race, however, the Formula One qualifying grid was dominated by cars using Michelin tyres. Michelin took a dim view of drivers of teams to which it supplied tyres giving free publicity to its arch Formula One rival Goodyear. Goodyear supplied the tyres for the M1 and forbade

Gilles Villeneuve, Jody Scheckter, René Arnoux and Jean-Pierre Jabouille from taking part in the event.

Even so, regulars in the so-called Procar series included the likes of Niki Lauda, Nelson Piquet, James Hunt, Alan Jones and Mario Andretti, all of whom had been, or were shortly to become, Formula One world champions.

None of this could disguise the sad truth that the M1 racing car was obsolete almost before it turned a wheel and that the only real chance it had of winning an important sportscar race was to make sure no other makes entered. So while BMW gained some undoubted kudos from the Procar project and salvaged the racing M1 at the same time, few were too surprised when after two short seasons, Procar racing ceased and the M1, as a competitive racing entity, was consigned to the history books.

It is hard to believe that the M1 road car started life as a racing-car project that went horribly wrong. The brain-child of Jochen Neerspach, the original plan was for the car to have been produced by Lamborghini, but when the Italian marque struck yet more of its famous financial woes the entire operation was removed back to Germany. The racing cars that did finally appear became legends.

Bugatti EB110

When history comes to recall those notable road cars that had the single greatest talent for turning their manufacturers' bank statements from black to red, it will be those such as the Bugatti EB110 that will be most frequently cited.

Built with a magnificent V12 engine with a capacity of 3.5 litres, and with 60 valves and four turbochargers producing, in SuperSport specification, an eye-watering 610bhp, it had a power plant truly worthy of one of the greatest names in prewar motor racing. Better still, its four-wheel-drive chassis was designed by Mauro Forghieri, whose curriculum vitae included the design of World Championship-winning Formula One Ferraris.

It should have looked great, too, styled by Marcello Gandini, the man responsible for such landmark shapes as the Lamborghini Countach and Lancia Stratos. Its troubles

started at its launch, when the covers were lifted and the attendant paparazzi and glitterati were presented with a slab-sided, shovel-snouted car that seemed to draw little from the legend of the great French company whose name it had bought.

If only the critics had been allowed to drive it. Of all the supercars produced in Italy in the last decade, only the Ferrari F40 provided the same sort of focus as the EB110SS. Possessing more power and considerably less weight than the softer, standard EB110GT, with its mere 553bhp, the SS, or SuperSport, provided me with one of the most memorable driving experiences of my life.

It feels right from the moment you snap shut the scissor-type door and cocoon yourself in its cabin. You note the rev-counter and spot the rev-limit way up at 8,500rpm. Turn the key, the engine catches and settles down to an even, rumbling idle. Check the mirror and you realize all you can see is the top of the perspex-covered engine. As far as rear visibility is concerned, you might as well be driving an HGV. Blip the accelerator pedal and you see the banks of throttle-bodies, synchronized, snap open and closed. Then you move off.

Below 4,500rpm, an Escort driver would need to take care not to run into the back of you. Then, as the needle passes this point, you need to be listening for the whoosh – it's all the warning you get. What happens next is not acceleration in any conventional sense, more of a uni-dimensional explosion in which the entire force is sent in one direction with you sitting on top. Thanks to the four-wheel drive, there is no wheelspin and, briefly, it seems to be all and more than you can do simply to change gear in time before the engine hits the red.

It takes a great deal of acclimatization and more than a little skill if it is to be driven within that very narrow band between embarrassingly slow progress and Armageddon. Even so, once you have mastered the elements of driving the Bugatti, refining the technique is remarkably easy. For one of such power, it is, in fact, an extraordinarily safe car to drive fast. For a start, its road-holding and grip are rather more impressive than its acceleration. Finding the limit in the dry on the public road is a suicidal waste of time. So deep are its reserves of grip that corners, which every cell in your body screams at you to slow down for, can be taken with unabated speed. And, if you need to stop, I have never driven another car that will do it quite like this Bugatti.

All of this was not enough to save the company. It paid for the sin of building a car that went a hundred times better than it looked and went into liquidation in 1995. Less than a hundred cars had been built.

Overleaf: The scissor doors worked well unless you turned the car over and had to get out.

A wedgy profile reveals no hidden beauty. The stylist claims also to have done the Lamborghini Miura.

The Bugatti's cabin worked well if you were less than about 175cm (5ft 9in), otherwise it could be excruciatingly uncomfortable, especially in its GT form. Its rearward visibility was also appalling and, thanks to the flexed rear spoiler, literally non-existent in the SuperSport.

Bugatti EB110

Manufactured: 1994-95
Number of cars: c30

Dimensions
Length: 4,400mm
Width: 1,940mm
Height: 1,125mm
Wheelbase: 2,550mm
Front track/rear track: 1,555mm/1,620mm
Kerb weight: 1,566kg

Engine
Capacity: 3,500cc
Bore/stroke: 81mm/57mm
Construction: Aluminium head,
   aluminium block
Valve gear: 5 valves per cylinder, dohc
Compression ratio: 7.5:1
Max power: 611bhp at 8,250rpm
Max torque: 479lb ft at 4,200rpm
Gearbox: 6-speed manual

Brakes
Front: Ventilated discs
Rear: Ventilated discs
Servo assistance/anti-lock: Yes/yes

Suspension
Front: Double wishbone, coil springs,
   anti-roll bar
Rear: Double wishbone, coil springs,
   anti-roll bar

Steering system
Power-assisted rack and pinion

Wheels and tyres
Wheel size: 9.0 x 18in (f), 12.0 x 18in (r)
Construction: Alloy
Tyre size: 245/40 ZR 18 (f), 325/30 ZR 18 (r)

Claimed performance
0-97kph (0–60mph): 3.3sec
Max speed: 322kph (200mph) plus

This engine is an automotive miracle, with 12 cylinders, four camshafts, 60 valves and no less than four turbochargers. However, this potential nightmare recipe proved not only to be explosively powerful but also strong and reliable.

The story of Bugatti's second, and ultimately doomed, attempt to re-establish itself as one of the world's finest car makers is the story of one Romano Artioli. Far from being a descendant of, or in any way connected or related to, the great Ettore Bugatti, Artioli is a maverick Italian businessman who simply bought the rights to the Bugatti name.

He hired the finest designers and built one of the most striking car factories in the world, on the *autostrada* that runs north out of Modena. Here, despite not being in Bugatti's native France, the company would at least be able to bask in the glory reflected from its neighbours at Ferrari, Maserati and Lamborghini.

Sadly, the timing was all wrong and, like the McLaren F1 and Jaguar XJ220, the car was finished at a time when people who had spent and lost millions on fast cars when the late eighties' boom collapsed were still licking their wounds. Pumping huge quantities of cash back into a car with no track record whatsoever, and distinctly controversial looks, was, perhaps, not too high on many of their agendas.

The budding Formula One ace, Michael Schumacher was one who did take the plunge, taking delivery of a SuperSport but, in the main, it failed to attract the same quantities of big names that, just a few years earlier, would doubtless have been falling over each other to buy a brand new car with such an emotive badge.

One of Artioli's brighter moves during his time at Bugatti was to buy Lotus Cars from General Motors, which had an extremely able and well-respected consultancy business. It was during his tenure that the brilliant Elise sportscar was produced and named after Artioli's granddaughter.

Being on the road in a Bugatti SuperSport was one of the rarest delights of all. Of all modern supercars, only Ferrari's F40 provided the same dedication to driving pleasure at the expense of everything else.

Aston Martin DB7

The most beautiful car of the 1990s? Many believe this title belongs to the DB7, with its brilliant blend of modern purpose and traditional Aston Martin styling.

It may seem odd but without Jaguar the Aston Martin DB7 would probably never have been built. What Jaguar and Aston Martin have in common is their parent, Ford, and what Jaguar had and Aston Martin needed desperately, was the basis of a new sportscar. Jaguar would have called it the F-type, but when the decision was made to make a new car – rather than one based on the old XJS – the F-type was initially shelved and then given to Tom Walkinshaw's TWR organization to turn into the best Aston Martin that had been seen for 30 years.

There are those who say, therefore, that the DB7 is no Aston Martin at all. Powered by a supercharged, 3.2-litre Jaguar engine, on a modified XJS platform and built by TWR nowhere near Newport Pagnell but, instead, in the same factory that had hitherto been turning out Jaguar XJ220s, it is easy to see their point.

Except that none of this matters. The DB7 looks like an Aston Martin and, rather more importantly, it goes and feels like one, too. The supercharger has done rather more than provide 330bhp, it has given the engine an identity utterly removed from any variant fitted to a normally aspirated Jaguar, as well as considerably more power. Its noise is that of the classic British straight six, overlaid by the haunting offbeat hum of the supercharger.

And thanks to the supercharger's greatest benefit, the ability to provide surging power at any engine speed you like, the DB7's performance is as relentless as you would hope for from a car wearing the proud Aston Martin wings. It will fling the DB7 past 97kph (60mph) in rather less than 6 seconds and up to a top speed on the far side of 257kph (160mph).

Indeed, the only area in which it feels quite unlike its stable mates is the attitude it displays towards corners. Astons have, within certain limits, always handled well.

The DB7 does away with these limits altogether. Using the knowledge and expertize learned on the racetracks, from Le Mans to Formula One, TWR's engineers have produced a chassis of rare quality, one that grips hard, provides exemplary body control, yet suspends its occupants on a cushion of comfort that is seemingly quite at odds with such finely honed handling. It takes just a few minutes at the wheel to marvel that such a chassis could bear any relation to that of the capable, but hardly ground-breaking, XJS.

Yet, on the inside, the influence of its parent has not been removed entirely. On the contrary, in its driving position, strangely lacking in leg room for a car of such generous dimensions, the signature of the XJS remains. It is a shame since, in all other respects, from the appropriate use of

wood to the deep luxury of its Connolly leather, the DB7 feels every inch the pure-bred Aston Martin.

And it looks it. Its lines were penned by one Ian Callum, working not for Aston Martin but, once more, for TWR. What he achieved was the finest looking British sportscar since the E-type was launched in 1961, and what remains is perhaps the most attractive car on sale today. Given that so many of the determining factors of the shape were imposed by the limitations of the XJS platform, the scale of the achievement is all the more remarkable.

The DB7 came at a time when Aston Martin was in deep crisis. Having been forced into asking Ford to take over the company, it was faced with a car that, if it had not succeeded, would have spelled certain death. In fact, Aston's future now looks stronger than ever, and for that it has the DB7 alone to thank.

Overleaf: A DB7 is no poseur's car. It responds well to being driven in anger thanks to its capable yet comfortable chassis.

When seen from any angle, the DB7 looks good, thanks to the talent of stylist Ian Callum. The dinner-plate wheels work particularly well.

Aston Martin DB7

Manufactured: 1994-2004
Number of cars: 7,091

Dimensions

Length: 4,631mm
Width: 1,820mm
Height: 1,268mm
Wheelbase: 2,591mm
Front track/rear track: 1,524mm/1,530mm
Kerb weight: 1,650kg

Engine

Capacity: 3,239cc
Bore/stroke: 91mm/83mm
Construction: Aluminium head,
    aluminium block
Valve gear: 4 valves per cylinder, dohc
Compression ratio: 8.3:1
Max power: 335bhp at 5,500rpm
Max torque: 360lb ft at 3,000rpm
Gearbox: 5-speed manual

Brakes

Front: Ventilated discs
Rear: Ventilated discs
Servo assistance/anti-lock: Yes/yes

Suspension

Front: Double wishbones, coil springs,
    anti-roll bar
Rear: Lower wishbones, coil springs,
    upper links, anti-roll bar

Steering system

Power-assisted rack and pinion

Wheels and tyres

Wheel size: 8.0 x 18in
Construction: Alloy
Tyre size: 245/40 ZR 18

Claimed performance

0–97kph (0–60mph): 5.7sec
Max speed: 266kph (165mph)

It says Aston Martin on the engine but do not be fooled by this. It is a Jaguar power plant, albeit considerably modified and supercharged for the DB7.

Opposite: The driving position still shows signs of the Jaguar XJS, from which the DB7 was derived. There is not enough leg room for those much over 1.8m (6ft). The leather interior trim is, however, impeccable.

Thankfully, the Aston Martin DB7 will not be remembered as the car James Bond rejected in favour of his trusty old DB5 and, curiously, a BMW Z3, but it is true that Aston Martin, like Lotus, offered cars for the *Goldeneye* film and both were turned down.

This does not, however, mean that the DB7 was in any way short of famous faces queuing up to slip behind the wheel. Stirling Moss seemed converted on the spot, commenting: 'What a beautiful car the DB7 is! But for me the most important thing is that it's still essentially an Aston Martin. It's typically Aston in the best way: it looks good, it's smooth, it's fast. It's enjoyable to drive and very driver friendly.'

Sports personalities seem particularly taken by the charms of the DB7 with Ryan Giggs, Ian Wright and David Platt all leaping at the chance of owning one of these machines, as did the ex-captain of the England Rugby Team, Will Carling. The royal family seems similarly keen to continue its old association with the marque, with both Prince Andrew, Duke of York, and avid car fan Prince Michael of Kent choosing DB7s for their transport.

The DB7 also marked Aston's first tentative steps back towards competitive track work, a tradition started by a prototype Aston Martin back in 1919. There has been just one DB7GT built so far, a car very much in the traditions of the much loved DB4GT – although, to date, it has not been developed to a state where it could win an important series. Indeed, it was apparently never intended to be a race winner, more of a showcase for the competition potential of the car as well as a way of making trackwork altogether more civilized. For all its racing intent, it still has leather seats.

On the road in the most successful Aston Martin in its history. Single-handed, it saved the company.

Porsche 959

A Porsche 959 will not travel at quite 320kph (200mph). Given an ideally endless strip of tarmac, though, and it will run through its six gears right the way up to about 315kph (196mph) or, some say, even to 317kph (197mph). Not bad, but nobody has ever suggested that the 320kph (200mph) barrier is on the cards. What is surprising is that the reason the 959 will not reach the magic 320kph (200mph) mark is that Porsche felt there simply was no need for it. Had the company so decided, it would have made short work of adding those last few inches of speed – but, no, 317kph (197mph) was enough.

Porsche, of course, was correct in making this policy decision. The importance of such velocities is almost entirely academic and the 959 was never designed as a car to be theorized over. It was designed, like the 911 upon which it was based, to be used.

This did not stop the 959's performance causing superlative melt-down among those who were the first lucky enough to drive it. Arriving before even the Ferrari F40 had broken cover it was, for a short while at least, massively faster than anything else currently on the road, eclipsing the 303-kph (188-mph) Ferrari 288GTO with ease. Moreover, thanks to its four-wheel-drive system, anti-lock brakes and a superb six-speed gearbox, it achieved this level of performance with a style and greater sophistication than any other car that had ever been built. It was a techno-logical *tour de force*.

Which meant that while a Ferrari 288GTO would reach, say, 274kph (170mph), the 959 would fly to such a speed in an instant and, if required, main-tain that rate of travel without the slightest sign of effort, thundering on and on until its fuel tank ran dry. When motoring journalists recall extraordinary trans-European road journeys completed in times that seem unachievable, more of them seem to have been completed in Porsche 959s than in any other car.

The heart of this most civilized of beasts was yet one more turbocharged derivative of Porsche's well-tried and enduring flat-six engine. The 959's 2.85-litre capacity was actually less than the 3.2 litres of the standard 911 model thanks to extant race regulations that compensated for the extra power produced by a turbocharger by multiplying engine capacity by a factor of 1.4, deeming the 959's capacity to tuck in just below the 4-litre limit. This did not prevent it providing more than enough power to get the job done.

While a stock 911 of the era, still a quick car even by today's standards, possessed 231bhp, the 959 boasted nearly twice as much with a cool 450bhp. Harnessed to the traction of the four-wheel-drive system the engine provided a 0-97kph (0-60mph) capability of rather less than 4 seconds, a feat that, at the time, seemed impossible right up to the moment that it was realized the 959 would do it again and again without ever raising a sweat. Instead, the only thing it raised was the collective heart rate of its audiences.

In less extreme driving circumstances, the 959 behaved with at least the civility of the 911. As long as you remembered to keep your right foot well away from the floor, the car would trundle through traffic with the best of them, provide excellent visibility, considerable comfort, admirable refinement and many admiring stares. Even when you kicked the throttle wide open,

Overleaf: In its day, nobody had ever come across a device that was as devastatingly efficient on twisting roads as the 959.

The outline of the 911, upon which the 959 is based, is clear from this profile shot. The doors are identical.

Porsche 959

Manufactured: 1987-88
Number of cars: 200

Dimensions
Length: 4,260mm
Width: 1,840mm
Height: 1,280mm
Wheelbase: 2,300mm
Front track/rear track: 1,504mm/1,556mm
Kerb weight: 1,350kg

Engine
Capacity: 2,850cc
Bore/stroke: 95mm/67mm
Construction: Aluminium head,
   aluminium block
Valve gear: 4 valves per cylinder, dohc
Compression ratio: 8.3:1
Max power: 450bhp at 6,500rpm
Max torque: 369lb ft at 5,000rpm
Gearbox: 6-speed manual

Brakes
Front: Ventilated discs
Rear: Ventilated discs
Servo assistance/anti-lock: Yes/no

Suspension
Front: Double wishbones, coil springs,
   anti-roll bar
Rear: Double wishbones, coil springs,
   anti-roll bar

Steering system
Power-assisted rack and pinion

Wheels and tyres
Wheel size: 8.0 x 17in (f), 10.0 x 17in (r)
Construction: Alloy
Tyre size: 235/45 VR 17 (f), 255/40 VR 17 (r)

Claimed performance
0-97kph (0-60mph): 3.9sec
Max speed: 317kph (197mph)

there would be this considered pause, as the revs gently rose, before the turbo boost kicked into play, rocketing the car forward. And even then, the savage punch in the kidneys that followed this acceleration was delivered with such little fuss and noise, and with such deft precision, that it still seemed hard to reconcile the figures you were reading on the speedometer with your perceived rate of progress.

There are some people who say that the 959, in its single-minded pursuit of technological perfection, left the driver too far out of the equation, and it is true that, compared with some other of the dream cars here, it proved less involving than its performance would suggest. As the ultimate cross-continent express, however, it would not be until the advent of the McLaren F1 that anyone did it better.

The cliché goes that you can tell a lot about a person from the car he or she drives. But on those few occasions when the owner is actually even more famous than the car, what is little understood is that precisely the reverse is also true. It speaks volumes about the car.

One of the very first 959s, and one of only a dozen ever to be brought officially into the UK by Porsche's British importers, was collected from the factory and driven straight to the front door of Olympic gold-winner Daley Thompson.

In his day, Thompson was far and away the finest decathlete in the world and one of the greatest athletes of any era, and it was perhaps not surprising that he should choose to drive what was then not simply the fastest car money could buy but also one of the strongest, most agile and effective cars in all conditions that could be conceived. Just as a decathlete needs to be able to turn in world-beating performances in several different disciplines, so the Porsche 959 did the same.

The 959 managed this world-beating performance by turning a well-worn principle on its head. This said that road-car engines could, if suitably modified, be installed successfully in racing cars, but that racing-car engines could not be successfully installed in road cars. But by taking the engine from the Porsche 962 – the most successful sports racer of all time – and mildly detuning it for the requirements of road use and to allow it to run on ordinary road fuel, Porsche was able to provide an engine whose reliability and power had been tested to the limit on all the major racetracks around the world.

Thanks to its hardly dainty waistline and heavy four-wheel-drive system, the 959 was never intended for serious track use itself, but this did not prevent specially converted examples from romping to first and second places in the 1989 Paris-Dakar rally.

Previous spread: The 959's mighty engine owes more to the all-conquering Porsche 956/962, perhaps the most successful sports racing car of all time, than the road-going 911. It produced an easy 450bhp, while the racers developed 650bhp, and rarely, if ever, went wrong.

Its cabin is taken more or less straight from the 911, although extra read-outs were needed to show the configuration of the very complex four-wheel-drive system. Today's 911 Turbo has a much simpler four-wheel-drive system and it works rather better.

Aston Martin DB5

There is one thread, one factor, that alone explains the entire and massive appeal of the Aston Martin DB5. It is its Englishness. There are many things England does badly and many things for it to be ashamed of in its past, present and, no doubt, future. But there is a certain effortless elegance in certain things the English build that is equalled nowhere else in the world. And of all the wondrous cars produced by England's multitude of specialist car manufacturers over the years, perhaps none expressed these values better than the Aston Martin DB5.

The DB5 is no sportscar; it is the ultimate GT car of the 1960s. There was nothing particularly modern about its bodywork, especially if you stood it next to the older but much further forward thinking Jaguar E-type, but Aston Martin has always resisted the urge to create advanced shapes. These considerations play no part in such

an understated and urbane creation as the DB5. It is happy instead with the simpler fact that it is quite beautiful and that its often complex curves work to perfection from stem to stern in a way that no Aston would emulate until the launch of the DB7.

The theme continues on the inside, where flashy touches are conspicuous only by their absence. There is a typically huge steering wheel, elegant but spidery instruments laid out in regimented order across the dash and exquisite switchgear. Every switch and button has a precision and an action that reeks of class. In not the smallest detail does the DB5 allow the essence of its Englishness to be compromised. In its upholstery and leather, you would need a Rolls-Royce before stumbling across another that understood the subject so well.

The engine, of course, is a massive twin cam, straight six, though, oddly, it was designed by a Pole, a genius called Tadek

Marek, who started working for Aston Martin by modifying the WO Bentley-designed six used from the end of the war until 1959, and then went on to create the 5.3-litre V8 motor that remains in use today. With 4 litres and up to 280bhp, it would propel the DB5 to close to 240kph (150mph). Even that, though, was not the point, since the cheaper E-type had claimed to have passed that point four years before. The DB5's point, and where it did score over the Jaguar, was in the effortlessness of its performance, the way it would deliver its driver unruffled to the south of France after many hours at 210kph (130mph).

As a device to be hurled around, the DB5 had distinct limitations. By the mid-1960s, Aston Martin had shifted away from racing and the road cars made a parallel move towards the more civilized pursuit of providing easy touring. So while the DB5

moved through corners with some authority and no little competence, the agility of its lighter and more lithe predecessors was compromised. A quasi-racing car it most certainly is not.

Treat it with respect, though, guide it through curves rather than chucking it around corners and its true class soon becomes apparent. This is a car of real pedigree and the way it flows effortlessly along a twisting road is evidence of this as solid as that coming from the smooth engine roar or the precise engagement of each of its five gears.

In a nutshell, the DB5's achievement is that it is the car that best combined the excitement of Jaguar without its brashness and the class of a Rolls-Royce without its stodge. It was the quintessential British touring car of its time and one of the finest GTs the world has known.

Overleaf: The DB5 looked less modern than the older Jaguar E-type, but it is no less pretty. Its styling was a landmark in British car design.

This is where the DB5 is at its best, cruising all day at high speed and with surprising comfort. For its time, it was quick, too.

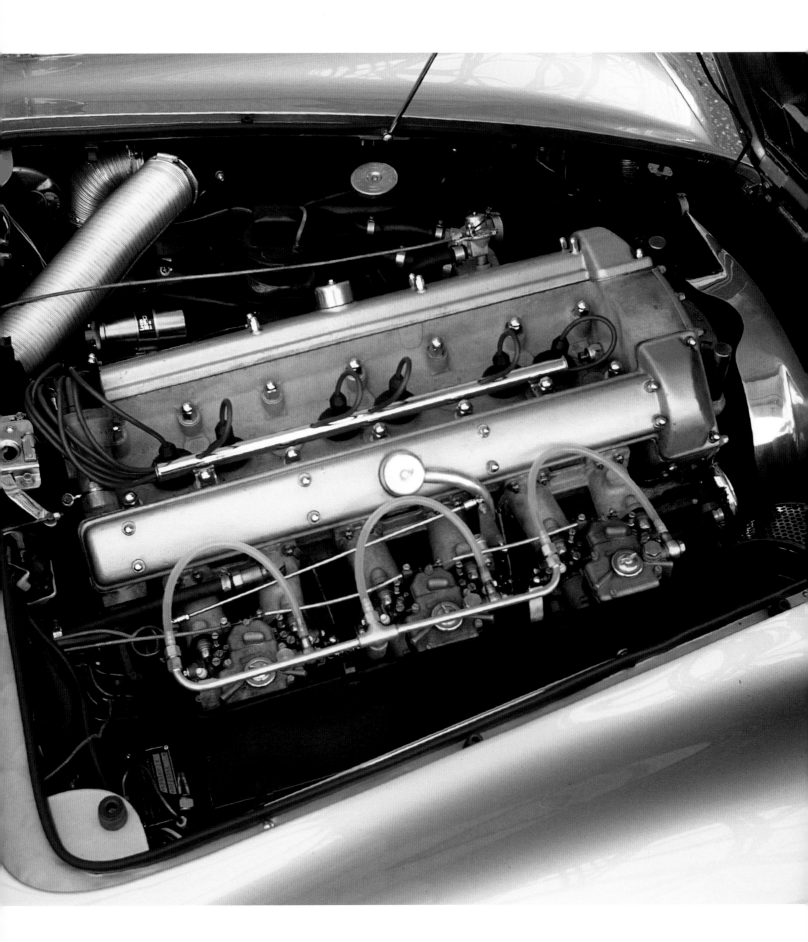

Aston Martin DB5

Manufactured: 1963-65
Number of cars: 1,022

Dimensions
Length: 4,458mm
Width: 1,674mm
Height: 1,334mm
Wheelbase: 2,489mm
Front track/rear track: 1,371mm/1,359mm
Kerb weight: 1,502kg

Engine
Capacity: 3,995cc
Bore/stroke: 96mm/92mm
Construction: Cast-iron head, cast-iron block
Valve gear: 2 valves per cylinder, dohc
Compression ratio: 8.9:1
Max power: 282bhp at 5,500rpm
Max torque: 280lb ft at 4,500rpm
Gearbox: 5-speed manual

Brakes
Front: Plain discs
Rear: Plain discs
Servo assistance/anti-lock: Yes/no

Suspension
Front: Double wishbones, coil springs,
    anti-roll bar
Rear: Live axle, trailing arms, coil springs

Steering system
Unassisted rack and pinion

Wheels and tyres
Wheel size: 5.5 x 15in
Construction: Steel, spoked
Tyre size: 6.70 x 15 crossplies

Claimed performance
0–97kph (0–60mph): 8.1sec
Max speed: 227kph (141mph)

Opposite: Its straight-six engine was designed by the engineering genius Tadek Marek. It first went into the DB4 in 1959 with a 3.7-litre capacity and 240bhp, rising to 4 litres and 282bhp for the DB5. With twin plug heads it went on to produce 314bhp for use in the race-derived, Zagato-bodied DB4GT.

The cabin uses the dash from the earlier DB2/4 MkIII and it works well. A huge wood-rimmed wheel is needed to keep the DB5 manageable.

The DB5 was made world famous when Sean Connery climbed aboard in 1964 for his third outing as secret agent James Bond in *Goldfinger*.

Fitted out by Q-branch with Boadicea wheel-spinners, machine guns, bullet-proof glass, a protective shield, tracking system, switchable number plates and that vital item in any government spy's automotive arsenal, the passenger's ejector seat, it made fine work of all baddies until being forced into a rather unconvincing brick wall.

In the books, as well as the original film, Dr No, the British agent, had relied on a Bentley for his wheels, but the charms of the just released Aston proved too much for the production company. And despite Bond finding himself over the years aboard, among others, a Ford, Toyota, Alfa-Romeo, and a couple of Lotuses it is the DB5 with which he remains most readily identified.

Thirty-one years later, the DB5 was back with Pierce Brosnan at the wheel in Bond's 16th adventure fantasy. Oddly enough, Aston Martin had offered the film makers, Eon Productions, its just released DB7 – a car seemingly tailor-made for the suave Mr Bond – but it was turned down in favour of the more traditional appeal of the DB5 and the extraordinary choice of a four-cylinder BMW Z3 roadster. Even so, Bond and the Aston were back on their usual neanderthal form, managing first to terrify and then to capture the affections of one young lady while simultaneously comprehensively out-driving another, despite the latter's seemingly insuperable advantage of being aboard a brand new Ferrari. Unsurprisingly she is involved in a plot to conquer the world and, as naturally as night turns to day, Bond conquers her, too. And then goes on to kill her. Of course.

Back in the early sixties, a view of the back was usually the only one you got if you spotted a DB5 on the road ... and even that view tended not to last for very long.

Lotus Esprit Sport 300

The Sport 300 was never one of the shy and retiring types, preferring instead bright paint and even brighter logos to announce its potential. It was not joking either.

The Lotus Esprit Sport 300 has an engine that sounds little better than a cement mixer and the sort of throttle response where, below about 3,000rpm, you would be quicker on the bus. Its gear change is hellish and its brakes undistinguished. It is difficult both to climb in and out of and, if you are over 1.8m (6ft), pretty uncomfortable once inside. All-round visibility is appalling, the dashboard is ergonomically dubious and the ventilation is a joke.

So what is it doing here? It is not even as if it can claim to be some paragon of beauty. Dramatic it may be, attractive, too, but with so many stuck-on wings, spats and spoilers the essential purity of Giugiaro's mid-1970s' shape has been all but lost.

No, there is just one reason why you are reading about the Sport 300 here: its handling. Lotus has, throughout its life, built cars riddled with faults. Some have been great, most have been good but a few have been poor. But if there is but one common thread running between them it is that every last one of them is among the best handling cars in the world.

Thus, the Sport 300 has been chosen to represent a breed of which it was, in its time, unquestionably the best. It was produced at a time when the Esprit was aged and in need of a star performer to prop up its well-worn act. Lighter and more powerful than any had gone before, it was extraordinary not simply for its mighty speed but also the fact that it was being produced by a 2.2-litre, 1960s' engine.

In fact, the engine was never going to do much more than set the chassis a few rather more challenging tasks. It rose to every one of them. To drive a Sport 300 fast for a couple of hours on deserted roads is to experience driving pleasure in as pure a form as you will find in a road-going supercar. It is a car that sharpens your senses until you can finally appreciate every nuance of the messages sent ceaselessly back to you through the suede rimmed steering wheel.

'You feel part of the car, as if yourself have become just an extension of the controls' is a sentence trotted out with tedious regularity by motoring journalists unable to think of anything more original to say about the way car and driver interact. There are but a handful of cars in the world actually deserving of such high praise, and the Sport 300 is definitely one of them.

Possessing the finest power steering ever created, it is ideal in weight, response, precision, gearing and feel. Moreover, its ability to supply desirable feedback, free of unwanted kickback, is unsurpassed. Add a chassis with truly astonishing levels of road grip and a ride quality that far from being firm and unyielding is soft and comfortable, and you can see why the purists seek out Lotus's Sport 300. A flawed diamond, for sure, but one that showed the world that there are still one or two areas of car design that call for more than just money.

Suede-rimmed racing seats are great, but the cabin lacks both head height and leg room. The dials are terrible, but the wheel is one of the best.

A Sport 300 at play on a private test track showing just how far it can be provoked without biting back. For all its many abilities, it was its stunning handling for which it became originally renowned, and for which it remains famous to this day.

OZ racing wheels not only look good but they were also light, critically keeping down the unsprung weight – which is one of the keys to a fine handling car.

Lotus Esprit Sport 300

Manufactured: 1994-95
Number of cars: 65

Dimensions

Length: 4,391mm
Width: 1,900mm
Height: 1,164mm
Wheelbase: 2,420mm
Front track/rear track: 1,533mm/1,594mm
Kerb weight: 1,306kg

Engine

Capacity: 2,173cc
Bore/stroke: 95mm/76mm
Construction: Aluminium head,
    aluminium block
Valve gear: 4 valves per cylinder, dohc
Compression ratio: 8.0:1
Max power: 302bhp at 6,600rpm
Max torque: 278lb ft at 4,500rpm
Gearbox: 5-speed manual

Brakes

Front: Ventilated discs
Rear: Ventilated discs
Servo assistance/anti-lock: Yes/yes

Suspension

Front: Double wishbones, coil springs,
    anti-roll bar
Rear: Double wishbones, coil springs,
    anti-roll bar

Steering system

Power-assisted rack and pinion

Wheels and tyres

Wheel size: 8.5 x 16in (f), 10.5 x 16in (r)
Construction: Alloy
Tyre size: 245/45 ZR 16 (f), 315/35 ZR 16 (r)

Claimed performance

0-97kph (0-60mph): 4.5sec
Max speed: 264kph (164mph)

This humble, four-cylinder motor started life as a normally aspirated 2-litre engine. It was stretched to 2.2-litres and fitted with a turbocharger for use in the original Esprit Turbo. Although the Sport 300 represented its ultimate on-road form, for racing the engine was made to give an astonishing 400bhp. Lotus replaced it with an all-new V8 engine, which was yet more powerful but, somehow, less full of character.

Lamborghini Diablo SV

The Diablo SV is a challenge to drive hard and should only be driven like this within the safety of a test track. Though it tends to behave unreasonably well, it is not a car for faint hearts or for the inexperienced driver.

That Lamborghini is alive today is something of a miracle. Beset by financial woes all its life, tossed from one owner to another and never provided with the budgets needed to properly exploit the talents and vision of its designers, its cars have too often relied on their speed, appearance and badge to draw a veil over their manifold limitations.

There are signs now, however, that Lamborghini has at last discovered a new sense of purpose and direction. It has realized that people who buy Lamborghinis do so for two reasons. There are those who wish to be seen in them, and those who wish to drive them. With only the ageing Diablo on the books, the company did the only thing it could: it chopped the

top off to make a roadster for those who wished to pose and beefed up the engine and stripped out the interior for those who chose to drive.

The Diablo Roadster is not a car I wish to comment on here, but the Diablo SV, the driver's car, most certainly is for it is the best Lamborghini to be built since the original Miura SV.

The Diablo SV is the last of the mammoth, mid-engined supercars of the 1970s. Even Ferrari's flagship is now a super-sophisticated, leather-lined express with its engine in its nose. The Diablo is not. Its 510bhp, 5.7-litre motor lives behind its driver and would propel the Diablo to 338kph (210mph) were it not geared down to provide maximum acceleration.

It is the most intimidating car made today, capable of invoking levels of trepidation not even a McLaren F1 or Ferrari F50 can induce. As you approach its upswung scissor door, you are aware of a massive car that dares you even to climb aboard, slither down behind the wheel and fire up the monster that occupies the entire rear section of the car. And if you do, you will discover something else: it's absolutely deafening.

Driving it is an exercise in restraint, in finding the right road, opening the throttles and feeling the bellowing V12 slam you back into your seat. Given space, it will go round corners at speeds most cars won't reach on the straights but you will be made to work for every inch of tarmac gained as you struggle to keep its massive bulk on line, operate the heavy gearbox and cope with its runaway performance. You reach the end of your journey both mentally and physically exhausted knowing you have just done several rounds with the most tiring, stressful and demanding supercar money will currently buy.

Picking holes in it is childishly easy: the interior is a joke, the air conditioning scarcely works, jumping in and out is a nightmare and rearward visibility hardly exists, but with the Diablo SV they are as nothing. The SV is a car that knows exactly its role in life. It is not for posing on the Riviera, it is for blasting over the mountains, demanding and rewarding in a way that few this side of a Ferrari F40 would comprehend.

The exposed gear-lever gate follows the Ferrari tradition right down to placing first gear on a dog-leg. The mighty gearbox handles the SV's power with disdain, slicing through its ratios with ease and gusto.

Lamborghini Diablo SV

Manufactured: 1996-1998
Number of cars: 346

Dimensions
Length: 4,470mm
Width: 2,040mm
Height: 1,115mm
Wheelbase: 2,650mm
Front track/rear track: 1,540mm/1,640mm
Kerb weight: 1,530kg

Engine
Capacity: 5,707cc
Bore/stroke: 87mm/80mm
Construction: Aluminium head,
    aluminium block
Valve gear: 4 valves per cylinder, dohc
Compression ratio: 10.0:1
Max power: 505bhp at 6,800rpm
Max torque: 427lb ft at 5,200rpm
Gearbox: 5-speed manual

Brakes
Front: Ventilated discs
Rear: Ventilated discs
Servo assistance/anti-lock: Yes/no

Suspension
Front: Double wishbones, coil springs,
    anti-roll bar
Rear: Double wishbones, coil springs,
    anti-roll bar

Steering system
Power-assisted rack and pinion

Wheels and tyres
Wheel size: 8.5 x 17in (f), 13.0 x 18in (r)
Construction: Alloy
Tyre size: 235/40 ZR 17 (f), 335/30 ZR 18 (r)

Claimed performance
0-97kph (0-60mph): 3.9sec
Max speed: 300kph (186mph)

Opposite: This huge, 5.7-litre V12 is one of the few magnificent power plants left in production today. It is extremely loud, even at idle, and snarls its way up to an inspiring bellow in short order when asked. Unlike other Diablos, the SV thankfully lacks the four-wheel-drive system, meaning that not only is the handling crisper but if you are in the mood to tear up money burning rubber in an orgy of tyre-squealing mayhem, the SV will also be only too happy to oblige.

Caterham Seven JPE

Anybody who drives a JPE without wearing a helmet is either very brave or unusually stupid ... stones thrown up from traffic mean that you can easily return home bleeding.

There are very few cars in the world that can match the JPE's acceleration – from rest to 160kph (100mph) in 13 seconds. What we are dealing with here is very possibly the maddest car ever offered for sale to the public. On its rev-counter there is a coloured warning band starting at 6,500rpm, but this is not the point at which the engine has given all it safely can, this is where the engine starts to get down to business.

Its power is extracted from a 2-litre Vauxhall engine, based on that in cars such as the Calibra 16v. Unlike the Calibra engine though, the JPE unit is tuned to full-race specification and produces 250bhp. But this is only half the secret. The other half is that it tips the scales at scarcely half a tonne. Which means that its accelerative abilities are no less than those you might find in a Calibra fitted with an engine from a F1 car.

The odd thing is, it feels even faster than it is. Because you sit so close to the ground, without even so much as a windscreen between you and the elements, none of the sensations of speed is damped out before reaching you. You can drive it wearing a flying hat and goggles, though a helmet makes much more sense and, as long as you stick below 6,500rpm, its performance is just about containable.

The realm above 6,500rpm is preferably sampled on the racetrack. Quite the best way to tackle the experience is to pretend it is not happening to you, that you are

merely instructing the driver to change gear here, point the car over there. It is a world where the previously furious acceleration becomes uniquely manic. Your senses are assaulted by the rush of the wind, the thumping suspension and the deafening attack of the engine. You don't seem to travel across the scenery so much as register your movements in a series of freeze-frames, each one more implausibly far away than the last.

But though this is a car that will accelerate faster than all bar the swiftest racing cars, it would be a mistake to escape with idea that it is simply an engine on wheels. Once you have learned to accommodate the acceleration (you never actually get used to it), you will learn that its real joy lies in its handling. Because it is so light, it does not take much to persuade it to change direction and the precision with which it does this will be a revelation.

The Seven JPE will make no sense to all bar a minority of people sufficiently skilled and similarly inclined to make the most of it.

It is hard to imagine how driving can be much more focused than this: no hood, doors or even a windscreen to come between you and the elements.

Caterham Seven JPE

Manufactured: 1993-2001
Number of cars: 50

Dimensions

Length: 3,100mm
Width: 1,575mm
Height: 800mm
Wheelbase: 2,225mm
Front track/rear track: 1,336mm/1,336mm
Kerb weight: 580kg

Engine

Capacity: 1,998cc
Bore/stroke: 86mm/86mm
Construction: Aluminium head,
    cast-iron block
Valve gear: 4 valves per cylinder, dohc
Compression ratio: 12.0:1
Max power: 250bhp at 7,750rpm
Max torque: 186lb ft at 6,250rpm
Gearbox: 5-speed manual

Brakes

Front: Ventilated discs
Rear: Plain discs
Servo assistance/anti-lock: No/no

Suspension

Front: Double wishbones, coil springs,
    anti-roll bar
Rear: De Dion axle, radius arms, coil springs
    anti-roll bar

Steering system

Unassisted rack and pinion

Wheels and tyres

Wheel size: 6.0 x 13in (f), 7.0 x 13in (r)
Construction: Alloy
Tyre size: 185/60 HR 13 (f), 205/60 HR 13 (r)

Claimed performance

0-97kph (0-60mph): 3.2sec
Max speed: 241kph (150mph)

Opposite: The open road in a Seven JPE is either one of the most hateful experiences anyone is likely to encounter or among the most incredible. How you respond depends on first, how much you like roller-skates with moon-rocket performance and, second, whether you are driving or not. There is no car in the world more frightening in which to be a passenger when driven fast. As a driver, though, the exhilaration at the end of even a very short run is nigh-on matchless.

Ford GT40 MkIII

There is a reasonably reliable rule of thumb that suggests that road cars do not make good race cars. What it does not make clear is that, unless completely re-engineered like some others on these pages, race cars invariably make simply appalling road cars.

The Ford GT40 MkIII is a truly terrible road car, so bad it became one of less than a handful with a credible claim to have been killed by a single press review. Just seven had been built. Certain modifications were needed to convert the multiple Le Mans winner into a road car, including higher headlights and a longer tail to provide space for a vestigial boot.

Today the most difficult part of driving the GT40 MkIII is climbing aboard. It is impossibly low, the steering wheel is huge and adept at snaring your feet as you try to slide down into the cockpit and there is less headroom than even in the racing version. And because the top of the door meets the car right in the centre of the roof, you run the risk of scalping yourself every time it closes.

Inside it is a pure sixties' racing car, apart from the inclusion of a speedometer. The engine, far from being an exquisitely crafted work of multi-valved wizardry, was just a lump of highly tuned Detroit iron with 4.7-litres and 306bhp compared with the 385bhp of the racing engine.

In 1967, it was just about the fastest thing you could buy, accelerating quicker than a Lamborghini Miura and reaching up to 274kph (170mph) in short and stable order. The noise, too, from the scarcely silenced V8 motor was incredible – a blaring, roaring explosion of energy greeting every blip of the throttle.

But despite all the magic, the list of what was wrong was long and ominous. The gearbox, converted from the racer to a central change, was a disgrace, the switch-gear was unfathomable and the ventilation was so bad that any journey on a hot summer's day was unadulterated torture. Rather worse was the fact that, to ameliorate the GT40's attitude to the everyday

lumps and bumps it would encounter in the big bad world, its racing suspension was softened and filled with energy-absorbing rubber. It had the feel of a race car but without the ability. Skinny, road-going tyres robbed it of grip and the beautiful poise and balance for which you long for from such a car was, sadly, nowhere to be seen.

The result was a caged lion, claws clipped and teeth blunted. It should probably never have been built – although, after a few miles in the cabin, it is hard to regret that it was.

Road modifications found on the GT40 MkIII included high wings and rudimentary bumpers.

The GT40's cabin is a nightmare. Hideously cramped, appallingly hot on a warm summer's day and boasting a gear-change of unusual recalcitrance.

The engine, however, is a fine example of humble Detroit iron being turned into a formidable road racing powerhouse.

Ford GT40 MkIII

Manufactured: 1968
Number of cars: 7

Dimensions
Length: 4,293mm
Width: 1,778mm
Height: 1,041mm
Wheelbase: 2,421mm
Front track/rear track: 1,402mm/1,402mm
Kerb weight: 1,062kg

Engine
Capacity: 4,736cc
Bore/stroke: 102mm/73mm
Construction: Cast-iron head,
    cast-iron block
Valve gear: 2 valves per cylinder, ohv
Compression ratio: 10.0:1
Max power: 306bhp at 6,000rpm
Max torque: 229lb ft at 4,200rpm
Gearbox: 5-speed manual

Brakes
Front: Plain discs
Rear: Plain discs
Servo assistance/anti-lock: Yes/no

Suspension
Front: Double wishbones, coil springs,
    anti-roll bar
Rear: Double wishbones, coil springs,
    anti-roll bar

Steering system
Unassisted rack and pinion

Wheels and tyres
Wheel size: 6.5 x 15in (f), 8.5 x 15in (r)
Construction: Steel, spoked
Tyre size: 5.5 x 15in (f), 7.0 x 15in (r)

Claimed performance
0-97kph (0-60mph): 5.5sec (estimated)
Max speed: 257kph (160mph) (estimated)

Though less beautiful than racing GT40s, the road-going, or MkIII, versions still boasted some lovely details, such as these scoops feeding air to the engine for power and to the rear brakes for cooling.

Jaguar XJ220

Never let it be said that the XJ220 lacked purpose. The car is even bigger in the flesh than it appears here, and it needs really wide open roads before its bizarre performance can be used to the full.

The Jaguar XJ220 was launched in 1988 to a rapturous reception. It was fitted with a mighty, 48-valve, V12 motor and a state-of-the-art four-wheel-drive system. It was the biggest monument to automotive excess the British had produced since the thirties.

When it finally reached production, things were no longer quite what they had been. The four-wheel drive was gone, and the V12 had been replaced by an engine with half the cylinders and not much more than half the capacity developed, it was alleged, from that found in the back of the MG Metro 6R4. But the most important thing that was missing was the boom time. Many who had placed orders cancelled, saying the car they were offered was not that which they ordered, while Jaguar counterclaimed in an effort to enforce the sales. Both financially and in public-relations terms, it was an utter disaster.

And yet it seems hard to see how those who ordered the car could really have felt shortchanged by the XJ220 that finally reached production. With 542bhp flooding out of its twin-turbo, V6 motor, not only would it reach 97kph (60mph) in a hitherto unprecedented 3.6 seconds, it would not stop accelerating until it hit 343kph (213mph). Jaguar removed the catalytic converters from one, bolted on some slick tyres for safety and ran it around a banked bowl until it went a few miles an hour faster.

It actually feels surprisingly civilized on the inside. The cabin is tastefully trimmed and the driving position exceptional. The engine sounds appalling but its capabilities should not be doubted. Yet even on full throttle, there is a certain lack of drama in the cabin. Certainly you are pinned back in your seat as both turbos cut in, but really the greatest sense of the speed accruing comes from watching the almost surreal rate at which the needle flicks around the speedometer.

On the road, this is a worrying trait. Because it feels so effortless, you find yourself approaching other cars at a rate that, if it does not frighten you, may well scare them. Even on quiet open roads when you are just trundling along, minding your own business, every time you look at the dials, you seem to be travelling faster than you had thought.

The XJ220 is a car with many faults. There is no luggage space to speak of, the gearbox is unpleasant and so steep is the angle of the windscreen it is impossible to drive safely towards a setting sun. Its handling, though, is magical in the dry, and its steering is simply sublime, heavy but flooded with feel. In the wet, though, it needs to be treated with great care.

I doubt the XJ220 will be remembered as a very good car. It was too big, too flawed and, above all, too late. History will, however, come to view it as a great car, the first of those cars for which 320kph (200mph) was just another number on the dial.

The XJ220's cabin is neatly trimmed but remarkably cramped for the car's size.

Jaguar XJ220

Manufactured: 1992-94
Number of cars: 265

Dimensions

Length: 4,860mm
Width: 2,000mm
Height: 1,150mm
Wheelbase: 2,640mm
Front track/rear track: n/a
Kerb weight: 1,350kg

Engine

Capacity: 2,498cc
Bore/stroke: 94mm/84mm
Construction: Aluminium head,
    aluminium block
Valve gear: 4 valves per cylinder, dohc
Compression ratio: 8.3:1
Max power: 542bhp at 6,500rpm
Max torque: 472lb ft at 5,000rpm
Gearbox: 5-speed manual

Brakes

Front: Ventilated discs
Rear: Ventilated discs
Servo assistance/anti-lock: Yes/no

Suspension

Front: Double wishbones, coil springs,
    anti-roll bar
Rear: Double wishbones, coil springs,
    anti-roll bar

Steering system

Unassisted rack and pinion

Wheels and tyres

Wheel size: 9.0 x 17in (f), 14.0 x 18in (r)
Construction: Alloy
Tyre size: 245/40 ZR 17 (f), 345/35 ZR 18 (r)

Claimed performance

0-97kph (0-60mph): 3.6sec
Max speed: 322kph (200mph) plus

Remarks that the XJ220's engine may not be entirely unrelated to that fitted to the MG Metro 6R4 rally car tend not to win friends at Jaguar. Whatever the truth, the 542-bhp, 3.5-litre motor packs the biggest punch this side of a McLaren F1. Sadly, it sounds rather more like a cement mixer than a thoroughbred supercar engine. The original plans included a quad-cam V12 engine, but these were dropped for production versions.

Opposite: The light fades on Wales's Black Mountain after a hard day's running on some of the best roads Europe has to offer a car as fast and as large as an XJ220. It is a breathtaking shape, styled by Keith Helfet, and fully in keeping with the gorgeous Jaguar sports cars of the post-war era.

Chrysler Viper GTS

The Viper is a big car and needs a lot of road and courage to drive really fast. It does behave itself quite well under such circumstances – as long as it has not been raining.

How big do you like your supercar engines? Honda has a 3-litre engine in its NSX, Ferrari uses 3.5 litres for its F355, while Porsche used 3.6 litres for the latest 911.

If you have trouble associating Chrysler with supercars, it will come as nothing compared with the shock of learning how big the engine is for its 306kph (190mph) monster – the mighty Viper GTS. It has 8 litres under its nose and is the world's only road-going V10-powered car.

The Viper is rather more awesome than it looks. Its engine was originally built for a Chrysler truck but, during Chrysler's brief ownership of Lamborghini, it was given the Italians to turn into a supercar engine. The result was an all-aluminium monster kicking out 450bhp and enough torque to change the rotation of the earth.

Its heritage is that of those superbly obvious muscle cars America produced before the oil crisis in the late 1960s and early 70s, and it is a tradition it sticks to while faithfully updating the concept.

The Viper is not subtle and sophisticated – it is an animal, lacking all the niceties of the latest supercars, such as anti-lock braking and traction control. In the Viper, these services are provided with your right foot alone and heaven help those who overdo it in the wrong conditions. For the Viper is a car of massive potential, out-accelerating all bar the very fastest and most expensive European supercars.

In the dry, it can be contained and driven both hard and safely by those quick witted and experienced enough to cope with its take-no-prisoners attitude to the open road. In such conditions, it is supremely involving, spitting you out at the end of a cross-country journey sweating and exhausted. When it is raining, though, it is a car to drive into its garage, lock the doors and forget about. There is no road car currently in production that is

more difficult to drive fast in the wet than a Viper. It is just plain frightening. It is to be enjoyed, therefore, on those fair days that come all year around in California, where it was designed.

Those who fall in love with Vipers, and there are rather more than the factory has the capacity to cope with, do so because in a world where almost all cars have been forced into accepting the compromises of life in the late 20th century, the Viper stands alone, two fingers aloft.

There is next to no space inside, it's a pig to drive in heavy traffic and its thirst for petrol is so huge that if it ever reached a mass audience it would be banned for depleting the world's supply of fossil fuel.

That will never happen. For even if the Viper were cheap, which it is not, it would remain a very particular car, one that appeals to only that tiny fraction of people who want their transport to fight back. To these people, the Viper GTS is not simply adorable, it is irreplaceable, too.

The Viper's cabin seems almost ridiculously low slung, but visibility is good. The gearbox came from a truck – it was all Chrysler had that could handle the power of the engine.

Chrysler Viper GTS

Manufactured: 1996-2002
Number of cars: 12,000

Dimensions
Length: 4,488mm
Width: 1,924mm
Height: 1,195mm
Wheelbase: 2,444mm
Front track/rear track: 1,514mm/1,538mm
Kerb weight: 1,535kg

Engine
Capacity: 7,990cc
Bore/stroke: 102mm/99mm
Construction: Aluminium head,
    aluminium block
Valve gear: 2 valves per cylinder, ohv
Compression ratio: 9.6:1
Max power: 450bhp at 5,200rpm
Max torque: 490lb ft at 3,900rpm
Gearbox: 6-speed manual

Brakes
Front: Ventilated discs
Rear: Ventilated discs
Servo assistance/anti-lock: Yes/no

Suspension
Front: Double wishbones, coil springs,
    anti-roll bar
Rear: Double wishbones, coil springs,
    anti-roll bar

Steering system
Power-assisted rack and pinion

Wheels and tyres
Wheel size: 10.0 x 17in (f), 13.0 x 17in (r)
Construction: Alloy
Tyre size: 275/40 ZR 17 (f), 335/35 ZR 17 (r)

Claimed performance
0-97kph (0-60mph): 4.5sec (likely)
Max speed: 306kph (190mph) (likely)

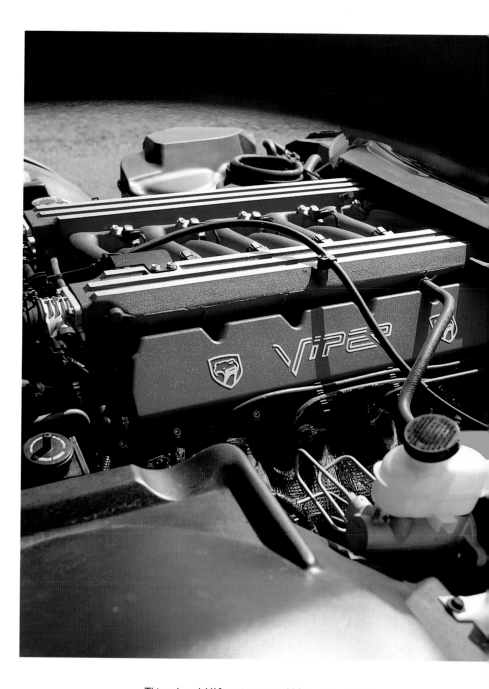

This colossal V10 engine started life in a truck before being given to Lamborghini (then owned by Chrysler) to be turned into something fit for a supercar. It was recast in aluminium and tuned to give 400bhp and, for the GTS, 450bhp. Despite its monstrous 8-litre capacity, it is docile until you prod the accelerator too hard.

Opposite: The Viper shape is one of the all time greats and heralds the return of the American muscle car. Its lines echo those of the Shelby Daytona Coupé from which evocative stripes have been borrowed.

Bentley Continental R

Few cars have genuine alter egos. Most are designed for a single purpose – to shop, cruise, race, carry heavy loads or large numbers of people. Of those few that do genuinely possess a split personality, the Bentley Continental R is perhaps the most appealing of all.

Unless you actively seek its secret side, the Continental R presents itself simply as one of the most satisfying ways of moving around the countryside. Despite its rakish coupé appearance, you sit imperiously high in the cabin, looking down on those in less fortunate machinery. The detailing of the cockpit is the finest of any car. The chromed organ stops that control the direction of the perfect air conditioning, the flawless acres of leather and the forest of timber on the dash are unlike those you will find in any other car. Best of all, oddly, are the carpets. The Continental R is a car many drive barefoot, cruise control on, both feet buried in the jungle of lambs' wool covering the floor.

In all, it is a pretty hedonistic way to go about your business. Under the bonnet lies a 6.7-litre, V8 engine that, because it is neither sufficiently quiet nor powerful without, comes with a turbocharger more usually found in lorries. Its best trick is to allow you to waft around the place, on a murmur of throttle, hoping you will not notice the rapidly plummeting fuel gauge.

To be honest, compared with the most modern Mercedes and BMWs, the Continental R is not even close in such crucial luxury car measures as ride and refinement. And if that shocks you, it should not. The Continental is based on a platform that was designed in the 1970s for a sum that would be regarded by Mercedes today as paltry. What matters rather more is that the Continental not only possesses a sense of quality and occasion that no other could imagine but also that, when the time comes, the Continental is also capable of the most outrageous behaviour.

If you see a Continental ambling along a country lane, do not presume it does so for any reason other than choice. Its engine possesses more torque, or sheer accelerative, than any other car in this book and if that is blunted by a 2.5-tonne weight, it's not by much. If asked, it will pick up its skirt and storm all the way to

241kph (150mph) and, were it not for its barndoor aerodynamics, far beyond that too. It is a strange feeling inside watching this exquisite drawing room on wheels sorting out Porsches.

Nor is it averse to being thrown around a bit. Its handling is hardly likely to rewrite any records, but point it at a twisting road and it will tackle it with considerable competence; a Ferrari it may not be but nor is it the wallowing barge.

In short, it is a Bentley, if not quite in the finest traditions of those that raced in the 1920s, then certainly as worthy an heir to the name of 'the silent sports car' as you will find. Packing looks, muscle and attention to detail in precisely the right quantities, it remains one of the all-important factors behind the on-going resurrection of this most fabled marque.

We have Ken Greenley and John Heffernan to thank for this wonderful shape.

Bentley Continental R

Manufactured: 1991 (on-going)
Number of cars: 1,120 (to date)

Dimensions
Length: 5,342mm
Width: 2,058mm
Height: 1,462mm
Wheelbase: 3,061mm
Front track/rear track: n/a
Kerb weight: 2,402kg

Engine
Capacity: 6,750cc
Bore/stroke: n/a
Construction: Aluminium head,
   aluminium block
Valve gear: 2 valves per cylinder, ohv
Compression ratio: 8.0:1
Max power: 385bhp at 4,000rpm
Max torque: 553lb ft at 2,000rpm
Gearbox: 4-speed automatic

Brakes
Front: Ventilated discs
Rear: Ventilated discs
Servo assistance/anti-lock: Yes/yes

Suspension
Front: Double wishbones, coil springs,
   anti-roll bar
Rear: Trailing arms, coil springs,
   anti-roll bar

Steering system
Power-assisted recirculating ball

Wheels and tyres
Wheel size: 7.5 x 17in
Construction: Alloy
Tyre size: 255/55 WR 17

Claimed performance
0-97kph (0-60mph): less than 6sec
Max speed: 250kph (155mph)

The Bentley Turbo motor is as old as the hills and it
will eventually be replaced by BMW engines. For now,
though, it is still the most torquey engine in production
thanks to its 6.75-litre capacity and colossal turbo. It will
not rev past 4,500rpm but it pulls like a locomotive
from idle. Twenty years ago, this engine was not rated at
all, today it is in danger of becoming one of the greats.

There is no more opulent car interior. The carpet is like
a jungle, the hand-stitched leather is unrivalled and the
use of wood, however politically incorrect, strikes a
tone of taste and civility unequalled by any other car in
production. The seats are superb and the attention to
detail second to none.

179

Ferrari F50

Seeing the F50 from this dead head-on angle is best. It oozes with purpose, if not exactly typical Ferrari beauty.

For all its achievements, Ferrari has been a notoriously conservative organization. It never chose to lead the field technologically, either in its road or racing cars. Rather, it preferred to see what the opposition was going to do and then decided either to ignore it or to do it rather better.

The F50's claim to fame is that it broke this mould and offered something to a few members of the general public that had never been seen in a road car before – a car based around a Formula One vehicle. McLaren's road car might have used a carbon-fibre chassis but even it stopped short of placing a Formula One engine under the hood. Not so Ferrari. The 4.7-litre, V12 motor in the F50 is a direct relation to the engine that so nearly won Alain Prost the World Championship in 1990. It has the same five valves per cylinder configuration and, like a Formula One car and unlike any other road car in history, it is bolted rigidly to the carbon-fibre monocoque.

The result is not, as you might expect, simply the fastest and the most scary road car ever invented. On the contrary, not only is the F50 less swift than its rival at McLaren, in a straight line it will not even keep up with the car it was designed to replace – the F40. None of this need matter, however. Ferrari did not play the Formula One card for outright speed, it wanted to use the technology to create a car that would be quicker point to point than any in its history.

And so it proves to be. Around a track, rather than down the straight, the F50 eliminates the F40, not simply because it has more grip but, remarkably, because it is so much easier to drive. With its big V12 doing the work without turbochargers there is no sudden bang of power to catch you unawares, just a constant surge whenever you want it, right up until it reaches its top speed of 321kph (200mph). Of all the cars capable of achieving such a velocity, the Ferrari F50 is by far the easiest to drive and the only one that you can simply climb aboard and drive quickly and safely without a long period of learning and familiarization.

Yet the car has its flaws. It is incredibly impractical, offering no luggage space worthy of a mention and nowhere to stow the huge, detachable roof. You either leave it at home and get wet if it rains, or take it along and drive with your head jammed

against it if you are unlucky enough to be 1.8m (6ft) tall or more.

Even so, its achievement is not to be underestimated, for it shows that Ferrari can lead as well as follow. And while it may not be the prettiest Ferrari ever created, technologically it is by far the most impressive. Whether its like has any future in this increasingly politically correct world is open to dispute. Right now we should simply be grateful that someone had the guts truly to take the lessons of Formula One and apply them to one of the most effective and impressive road cars of our times.

From this angle, F50 looks heavy handed and a long way from the traditionally gorgeous shapes we expect both from Ferrari and the F50's stylist, Pininfarina. The huge rear wing is needed at speeds of 325kph (202mph).

Ferrari F50

Manufactured: 1995-1996
Number of cars: 349

Dimensions

Length: 4,480mm
Width: 1,986mm
Height: 1,120mm
Wheelbase: 2,580mm
Front track/rear track: 1,620mm/1,602mm
Kerb weight: 1,230kg

Engine

Capacity: 4,698cc
Bore/stroke: 85mm/69mm
Construction: Aluminium head,
   iron block
Valve gear: 5 valves per cylinder, dohc
Compression ratio: 11.3:1
Max power: 513bhp at 8,000rpm
Max torque: 347lb ft at 6,500rpm
Gearbox: 6-speed manual

Brakes

Front: Ventilated discs
Rear: Ventilated discs
Servo assistance/anti-lock: No/no

Suspension

Front: Double wishbones, coil springs,
   anti-roll bar
Rear: Double wishbones, coil springs,
   anti-roll bar

Steering system

Rack and pinion

Wheels and tyres

Wheel size: 8.5 x 18in (f), 13.0 x 18in (r)
Construction: Cast magnesium
Tyre size: 245/35 ZR 18 (f), 335/30 ZR 18 (r)

Claimed performance

0-97kph (0-60mph): 3.7sec
Max speed: 325kph (202mph)

The F50 cockpit is remarkably civilized, with a good
driving position, a comfortable ride and a fine steering
wheel. Its electronic instruments are less successful.

Opposite: An F50 at large on Ferrari's private test track
at Fiorano, just around the corner from the factory.
Despite being slower in a straight line than the F40 it
succeeds, it is so much easier to drive and has such a
surfeit of grip that, around a track, it is convincingly the
quicker car.

Ferrari F355

On the road and travelling at speed is the F355 – the first of the junior breed of Ferraris to prove nearly as great as the first of all, the Dino 246GT. While the Dino had 195bhp, now the F355 produces 380bhp, or nearly as much as the Testarossa, Ferrari's flawed flagship of the mid 1980s.

Hard to believe though it may be, even Ferrari has its off days. All through the glorious decades of this greatest of sportscar marques you can see examples of cars that, had they not been wearing the famous prancing horse on their noses, would have been harshly criticized. The most recent example is the Ferrari 348, a car produced in the era just following Enzo Ferrari's death. It is a car that, despite its beautiful flowing lines and punchy engine, in no way honoured his memory.

Yet people only started to realize just what a poor Ferrari the 348 was when it was taken out of production and replaced by the F355, a visually similar but, in every way that matters, a massively better car. Whereas the 348 had 300bhp, the F355 had 380bhp, and while the 348 had five obstructive gears, the F355 boasted six sweet-changing ratios. The 348 had an

interior furnished from the Fiat spare parts bin, but by contrast the F355's cabin is bespoke Ferrari. In addition, the F355 had full underbody aerodynamics and an engine with not just five valves per cylinder but also an ability to rev higher than any other supercar in history, up to an astounding 8,800rpm if you really pushed it hard.

Yet the F355 was and is a pussycat compared with the 348. Despite its extra power and speed, the F355 is not in the least bit frightening to drive fast and, when you do make a mistake, you feel that the car is basically on your side. This same statement could not be said in defence of the 348, which proved no friend at all if you misjudged your cornering speed or hit an unexpected patch of wet road.

In fact, Ferrari made the F355 so good that many feared it would start to kill off their other models in the range. What point was there, after all, in buying a car like the twelve-cylinder 512TR when a 355 was prettier both inside and out, more fun to drive, faster point to point and, critically, many tens of thousands of pounds cheaper? In the end Ferrari avoided the issue by killing the 512 and designing its successor, the front-engined 550 Maranello, to be a Grand Touring kind of sportscar, not a little road racer like the F355.

Even so, the point remained valid. First, having created literally one of the worst cars in its history, Ferrari then chose to replace it with one of its, and the world's, best ever supercars.

When Ferrari decided, back in the mid 1960s, to add a second string to its bow and create a range of cheaper, more agile cars to complement its established range of continent-crushing twelve-cylinder models, the car it produced became known as the Dino 246GT, a car revered as much today as any other road car from the stable. What Ferrari could not then have known is that it would take the best part of a generation before it would find it a worthy successor. But, at last, in the F355, it finally has that car.

The F355 not only grips well, it also handles with a rare degree of forgiveness.

Ferrari F355

Manufactured: 1994 (on-going)
Number of cars: 3,000 (to date)

Dimensions
Length: 4,250mm
Width: 1,944mm
Height: 1,170mm
Wheelbase: 2,450mm
Front track/rear track: 1,514mm/1,161mm
Kerb weight: 1,422kg

Engine
Capacity: 3,496cc
Bore/stroke: 85mm/87mm
Construction: Aluminium head,
    aluminium block
Valve gear: 5 valves per cylinder, dohc
Compression ratio: 11.1:1
Max power: 380bhp at 8,250rpm
Max torque: 268lb ft at 6,000rpm
Gearbox: 6-speed manual

Brakes
Front: Ventilated discs
Rear: Ventilated discs
Servo assistance/anti-lock: Yes/yes

Suspension
Front: Double wishbones, coil springs,
    anti-roll bar
Rear: Double wishbones, coil springs,
    anti-roll bar

Steering system
Rack and pinion

Wheels and tyres
Wheel size: 6.5 x 18in (f), 10.0 x 18in (r)
Construction: Alloy
Tyre size: 225/40 ZR 18 (f), 265/40 ZR 18 (r)

Claimed performance
0-97kph (0-60mph): 4.6sec
Max speed: 298kph (185mph)

Yet another Ferrari mechanical masterpiece. Though
it is based on the V8 motor first seen in the 308GT4
of 1974, the F355 engine has changed almost out of
all recognition. Its specific output of 108bhp per litre
eclipses even that of the McLaren F1, and this is
achieved by using five valves (three intake, two outlet)
for each of its eight cylinders. Also, the engine has a flat-
plane crankshaft with 180-degree firing intervals, effectively creating two four-cylinder engines within a common block. This allows the engine to achieve much higher revs than a conventional V8, giving the F355 an
8,500rpm red-line, the highest of any supercar.

Porsche 968 ClubSport

The ClubSport feels at least as at home on the track as on the public road. Though mechanically similar to a standard 968, its lightweight construction transformed it as a driving machine.

The appeal of almost any Porsche is the brilliantly rounded package it provides. A Porsche is for flashing through the lanes, thrashing around tracks, crawling through traffic. No matter what you ask of it, it does it, and does it well.

Given this, it is odd to note that one of the greatest Porsches ever built was the one that bucked entirely this philosophy. The Porsche 968 ClubSport was no good at either huge motorway journeys or small forays into the urban jungle. It was too noisy and tiring for one, too uncomfortable for the other. Yet, unlike other Porsches, it had one talent so great that, during its heyday in the early 1990s, there

was not another on the road that, in this respect at least, could touch it.

Its simple but, to this day, scarcely ever matched, ability was to go around corners in such a manner that whoever happened to be behind the wheel felt like the most talented driver ever. It was, in its day, the very finest handling car money could buy.

It is not easy to say exactly what it was that conferred this talent on the 968 when it was converted to the lightweight, ClubSport specification. It was just one of those happy occasions where everything gels and the result is better than, you suspect, even its makers imagined. For a car that started life in 1975 as the Audi-built

Porsche 924 and was soon to die as space no longer remained for it within Porsche's product plan, this was a last laugh of mighty proportion.

That said, the elements had been there all along. A simple, strong four-cylinder engine sat in its nose and supplied a flood of easy power, while placing the six-speed gearbox underneath the floor of the boot gave perfect weight distribution. The rest was tuning the straight-forward, effective suspension into giving maximum control and making the car as light as possible.

The result was a car you drove with your fingertips, flowing through fast curves as if they did not exist, feeling all the time the unique communication link that it provided between you and road. It did that most difficult thing and seemed both stable and agile – swift enough to excite, sufficiently secure never to frighten.

And it never left you in any doubt that its spiritual home was the racetrack. Let loose, it would do things your head tells you cannot be done, recover the unrecoverable and, most incredible of all, provide equal satisfaction to its driver regardless of that person's ability.

It was hideously impractical, noisy and uncomfortable but when it was alone on an empty, twisting road, such thoughts could scarcely be further from your mind.

This rear shot shows how Porsche cleaned up the styling from the 944S2, on which it was based. The trick number plate comes courtesy of Porsche's UK importers.

Porsche 968 ClubSport

Manufactured: 1993-95
Number of cars: 1,371

Dimensions
Length: 4,320mm
Width: 1,735mm
Height: 1,275mm
Wheelbase: 2,450mm
Front track/rear track: 1,472mm/1,450mm
Kerb weight: 1,420kg

Engine
Capacity: 2,990cc
Bore/stroke: 104mm/88mm
Construction: Aluminium head,
   aluminium block
Valve gear: 4 valves per cylinder, dohc
Compression ratio: 10.0:1
Max power: 240bhp at 6,200rpm
Max torque: 225lb ft at 4,100rpm
Gearbox: 6-speed manual

Brakes
Front: Ventilated discs
Rear: Ventilated discs
Servo assistance/anti-lock: Yes/yes

Suspension
Front: Struts, coil springs, anti-roll bar
Rear: Semi-trailing arms, coil springs,
   anti-roll bar

Steering system
Power-assisted rack and pinion

Wheels and tyres
Wheel size: 7.5 x 17in (f), 9.0 x 17in (r)
Construction: Cast alloy
Tyre size: 225/45 ZR 17 (f), 255/40 ZR 17 (r)

Claimed performance
0-97kph (0-60mph): 6.1sec
Max speed: 248kph (154mph)

A 968 ClubSport on the original Nürburgring, the most
demanding racetrack in the world. With more than 130
corners peppered over 22.8km (14.2 miles) of purpose-
built racetrack, there is no greater challenge for a car.
The ClubSport copes with ease.

Opposite: Former Grand Prix star Dr Jonathan Palmer
proving that, with the right hands on the wheel, there is
just about nothing a ClubSport will not do if it is given
sufficient encouragement. In case you are wondering, of
course the car didn't spin.

Jaguar XK120

When the definitive history book of automotive endeavour finally comes to be written, the year 1948 will be remembered as a true vintage landmark for one event alone, for that was the year in which the Jaguar XK120 first saw the light of day.

Before the Second World War, the Jaguar company had existed as Swallow Sidecars, or simply abbreviated to SS as it was more commonly known. It had become famed for its stable of practical saloon cars and, in particular, the racy looking SS100 range of 2½- and 3½-litre sportscars. However, among the greats of the day, such as Alfas and Bugattis, Swallow Sidecars could not by any stretch of the imagination claim to be one of the world's leading sportscar manufacturers.

The introduction of the XK120 changed all that, along with the company name. The car's creators rightly figured that few customers in the immediate post-war era would prove eager to buy a car with an SS badge on its nose. What they created was not simply one of the most beautiful and memorable shapes of all time, they were also to provide the world with one of the most enduring, versatile and successful engines the world has ever seen.

At the time, few in England seemed keen to point out that the XK120's styling seemed to draw rather heavily on the influence of the pre-war BMW 328 – it was simply seen as a shape from heaven. And that it was. More enticing even than its styling or its appealingly low price was the 120mph (193kph) top speed hinted at in its name. Cars that could attain that type of speed had hitherto existed only within the artificial confines of the race-track, and so the fact that such power was available on the public road, and at a relatively affordable price, seemed scarcely believable to potential customers.

Which is as well because it is doubtful that any XK120 ever actually reached that speed without modification to the mechanics, aerodynamics or tyres. In the public's eye, though, it didn't matter any more than it mattered some 13 years later when all bar the most carefully prepared E-types failed to reach their claimed 241kph (150mph). The public's imagination had been caught and the name of the Jaguar car company was most definitely on the map.

And just because the XK120 was not quite as swift as it was claimed does not, for a single minute, suggest that the car was anything less that one of the quickest vehicles on the road at that time. With a brand new, twin-cam 3.4-litre engine pouring out its silken power, it would

flash past 160kph (100mph) with superb ease, while its handling provided more than enough competence to cope with the task.

It was, however, as the XK120C, or C-type, that this Jaguar did its company its greatest service. In 1951 it started Jaguar's success at the Le Mans 24-hour event with the first of seven victories and it came back in 1953 to win again not only as the first car to average more than 160kph (100mph) throughout the entire 24 hours of the race but also as the first car to win a race using disc brakes. It is hard to see how the new marque of Jaguar could have gained a better start.

It is hard to imagine the impact these lines had on post-war Britain. Its like had never been seen anywhere before.

Jaguar XK120

Manufactured: 1948-54
Number of cars: 12,055

Dimensions
Length: 4,390mm
Width: 1,570mm
Height: 1,360mm
Wheelbase: 2,590mm
Front track/rear track: 1,283mm/1,270mm
Kerb weight: 1,295kg

Engine
Capacity: 3,442cc
Bore/stroke: 83mm/106mm
Construction: Iron head, iron block
Valve gear: 2 valves per cylinder, dohc
Compression ratio: 8.0:1
Max power: 160bhp at 5,000rpm
Max torque: 195lb ft at 2,500rpm
Gearbox: 4-speed manual

Brakes
Front: Drums
Rear: Drums
Servo assistance/anti-lock: No/no

Suspension
Front: Double wishbones, torsion bar springing, anti-roll bar
Rear: Live axle, semi-elliptical leaf
springs

Steering system
Unassisted recirculating ball

Wheels and tyres
Wheel size: 6.0 x 16in
Construction: Steel, spoked
Tyre size: 6.0 x 16in

Claimed performance
0-97kph (0-60mph): 10sec
Max speed: 193kph (120mph)

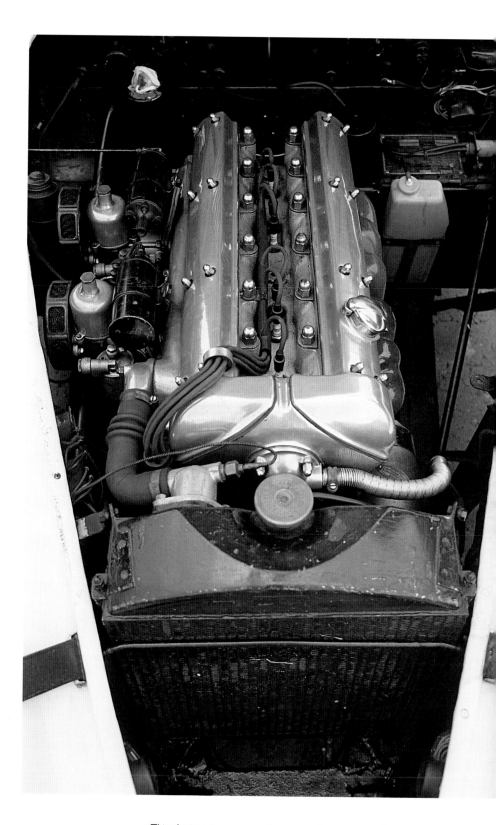

This glorious twin-cam engine was to become one of
the most enduring power plants of all time. In 1948, it
would push the Jaguar to 193kph (120mph) – a speed
that, before the war, would have been reserved for
racing cars alone.

Audi Quattro

The original Quattro was far from a thing of beauty, but beneath its slab-sided, boxy lines lay the makings of a legend and one of the most significant cars of our time.

It is only occasionally that a car comes along that makes the rest of the motor industry change the way it thinks about how it has built cars to date but, in 1980, that is exactly what the Audi Quattro did.

Until then four-wheel drive was a device employed entirely on such agricultural vehicles as Land-Rovers. Although this drive system was known to have certain traction advantages, giving a car four-wheel drive simultaneously made it heavier, slower and much thirstier. For these very telling reasons it had been ignored on all vehicles save those designed to go off-road, where there was a clear and obvious need for such a device.

Audi turned all that thinking on its head. Its Quattro was not some lumbering device, it was a smart coupé that was not simply devastatingly quick while the sun shone, it stayed that way when it rained,

too. With one single innovation, Audi made all of its rivals look inept in all bar ideal conditions. The Quattro was no fair weather friend, it kept going regardless, scarcely slowing down even when it snowed. It was the ultimate all-rounder.

So it is surprising to learn that there is nothing particularly clever about the Quattro. By using a turbocharged version of its 2.2-litre five-cylinder engine, it had the power to hit 220kph (137mph), but the four-wheel drive system equally split the power ratio between front and rear wheels. In this respect it was no more advanced than a Land-Rover even if, in later life, it did adopt an infinitely variable arrangement.

Then again, simplicity is the very substance of genius, and it was the way Audi took such conventional technologies and applied them that created a car so far ahead of its time and ensured its fame.

198

It was not a perfect car by any means. Its cornering ability in the wet may have been transformed but its braking remained distinctly conventional, creating what some saw as a chassis imbalance in those days before anti-lock braking came along. There was also a school of thought that suggested that this new four-wheel-drive system made drivers complacent and gave them a misplaced sense of immunity, tempting them to drive faster than otherwise they would and, in fact, merely raising the speed at which the car finally flew off the road.

To some extent this was true. The Quattro was a fine car but, like every other car ever produced, it was not foolproof. To most, however, this was not really the issue. What mattered more was that Audi had produced a car so far ahead of its rivals that soon it was being suggested that all cars would have to be made that way. In fact, it never happened. Four-wheel drive in road cars became popular for a while but, these days, manufacturers are tending more towards cheap, light, electronic devices such as traction control, rather than mechanical solutions for increasing the grip on a wet road. Even so, it did not stop the Quattro having its decade of fame as the most influential sportscar of the 1980s.

The Quattro was not just effortlessly quick, it was fast in any conditions you chanced across. And when the going got really tough, in the snow and sleet, for example, there was simply not another that could stay with it.

Audi Quattro

Manufactured: 1980-92
Number of cars: 9,944

Dimensions

Length: 4,404mm
Width: 1,703mm
Height: 1,344mm
Wheelbase: 2,524mm
Front track/rear track: 1,421mm/1,458mm
Kerb weight: 1,264kg

Engine

Capacity: 2,214cc
Bore/stroke: 80mm/86mm
Construction: Alloy head, iron block
Valve gear: 2 valves per cylinder, sohc
Compression ratio: 7.0:1
Max power: 200bhp at 5,500rpm
Max torque: 210lb ft at 3,500rpm
Gearbox: 5-speed manual

Brakes

Front: Ventilated discs
Rear: Ventilated discs
Servo assistance/anti-lock: Yes/no

Suspension

Front: Struts coil springs, anti-roll
bar
Rear: Struts coil springs, anti-roll
bar

Steering system

Power-assisted rack and pinion

Wheels and tyres

Wheel size: 6.0 x 15in
Construction: Cast alloy
Tyre size: 205/60 VR 15

Claimed performance

0-97kph (0-60mph): 7.3sec
Max speed: 220kph (137mph)

It may not seem like much, but you are looking at a landmark. The Quattro motor was remarkable not simply for the smooth 200bhp it produced from just 2.1 litres but also because it used five cylinders – a configuration that had historically been near impossible to make work in a petrol-powered car. Allied to an at first simple but then more sophisticated four-wheel-drive system, it made one of the most formidable drivelines of our time.

Chevrolet
Corvette ZR1

The ZR1 had very friendly handling, one that would allow you to get away with all manner of things a lesser car would have not forgiven.

Think of the Corvette and you are thinking of the archetypal American sportscar, an automobile designed to look good, go hard. The problem was that since the first examples of the breed appeared in the early 1950s, few had ever been able to perform in a manner commensurate with that suggested by their always outrageous appearance. And it was to answer this issue that General Motors, owners of Chevrolet, created the ZR1, the fastest and best Corvette in more than 40 years of near constant production.

Even so, it is perhaps indicative of the abiding limitations of American automotive engineering that Chevrolet chose to farm out the work required to turn its

everyday Corvette into the firebreathing ZR1 not to a specialist firm in the US but, instead, one in the UK – Lotus.

What Lotus did was to provide the Corvette with the punch it had always lacked. It took the standard 5.7-litre V8 that had powered millions of faceless GM saloons and went to work. By throwing away its inefficient pushrod-operated valve system and replacing the cylinder heads with new twin-overhead camshaft items, complete with four-valves per cylinder, it turned a trusty old nail into a muscle-bound powerhouse fit for a Porsche.

It was so powerful, it needed the gear-box from a truck to cope, and while this meant swapping ratios was not exactly the quickest of operations, it did at least mean that there were six to choose from, the tallest of which would propel you at 160kph (100mph) with just 2,000rpm on the clock. Indeed the ZR1 was so fast it included a switch that would shut down half the valves in the engine, cutting power by 100bhp should the owner not trust the driver with the full 375bhp.

It came with a chassis that could cope with such power. And by using some of the fattest tyres ever seen outside a race-track, the ZR1 would not simply cling on in corners, it could also be made to slide around at will thanks to the slow and friendly manner in which it would behave.

It continued to have its faults, of course, but these tended to add rather than detract from the character of the car. The interior, in particular, was an oasis of bad taste and ergonomic mismanagement. The dials were difficult to read, the switches were sprayed randomly around the dashboard and the cabin came swathed in some of the least pleasant shiny leather you can imagine.

Once you fired it up, however, these counted for little. What mattered most was, at last, here was an American car that was as truly amazing to drive as it was to look at. It was not until the Chrysler Viper came along that we saw its like again.

The ZR1 is most easily told from the more humble-looking Corvettes of the time by its restyled rear and smaller lights. The result was good looking and suitably brutal lines.

Chevrolet Corvette ZR1

Manufactured: 1990-95
Number of cars: 6,939

Dimensions

Length: 4,496mm
Width: 1,880mm
Height: 1,394mm
Wheelbase: 2,438mm
Front track/rear track: 1,524mm/1,575mm
Kerb weight: 1,573kg

Engine

Capacity: 5,727cc
Bore/stroke: 99mm/93mm
Construction: Alloy head, iron block
Valve gear: 4 valves per cylinder, dohc
Compression ratio: 11.0:1
Max power: 380bhp at 6,000rpm
Max torque: 375lb ft at 4,000rpm
Gearbox: 6-speed manual

Brakes

Front: Ventilated discs
Rear: Ventilated discs
Servo assistance/anti-lock: Yes/yes

Suspension

Front: Double wishbones, compound leaf
  springs, anti-roll bar
Rear: Upper and lower links, compound leaf
  springs, anti-roll bar

Steering system

Power-assisted rack and pinion

Wheels and tyres

Wheel size: 9.5 x 17in (f), 11.0 x 17in (r)
Construction: Cast alloy
Tyre size: 275/40 ZR 17 (f), 315/35 ZR 17 (r)

Claimed performance

0-97kph (0-60mph): 5.6sec
Max speed: 290kph (180mph)

The Lotus-developed, quad-cam, 32-valve engine was the key to the ZR1's success. It was capable of all manner of tricks, including shutting off half its valves and, therefore, providing only half the power when your teenage kid first asked to drive it around the block.

Opposite: Adult entertainment, Corvette-style. To achieve this effect, rev the engine to 7,000rpm, select first gear, drop the clutch and stand on the brakes while keeping the accelerator buried in the carpet. The car will eventually disappear altogether into the smoke. To be tried only by those on a test track who know exactly what they are doing. This is not for the faint-hearted or for anyone who has to pay for the tyres.

Lamborghini
Countach QV

Few words describe the lines of the Countach better than 'outrageous'. It was always designed to shock and it became the iconic supercar of the 1970 and early 1980s.

If you were a reader of car magazines through the 1970s and 80s, you will not have been able to avoid the Countach. So exciting to look at and so dramatic to drive was Lamborghini's wild child that, looking back, it seems that most of the more famous publications were stuffed with Countachs from cover to cover for the thick end of a decade.

It is not difficult to see why. For more than a decade, from its launch in 1973 to the arrival of the Ferrari 288GTO and Porsche 959 in 1984, it was perceived to be the fastest car in the world.

Whether this was actually true or not remains the subject of debate to this date. Italian performance claims of the early 1970s were not always among the most reliable statistics, and while some said that any old Countach would crack 290kph (180mph) without raising a sweat, others suggested something on the embarrassing side of 265kph (165mph) was nearer the mark, making the like of the Ferrari 365GTB/4, which was indisputably capable of 280kph (174mph), rather faster.

This is, of course, useful only if you are a fan of public-bar oratory. If the Countach was not always the fastest, then it probably held the title for longer than any other around at the time. The quickest version was not only the last but the best by some margin. Called the QV (for Quattrovalvole, heralding the fact that, at last,

the mighty V12 engine had received four valves per cylinder) it would probably punch a 306-kph (190-mph) hole in the air if you removed its monstrous rear wing and found a straight long enough and a sufficiently brave driver to have a go.

And, unlike so many cars whose driving experience fails to match the promise of their looks, the Countach was every bit as intimidating to drive as its mad appearance suggested. You sit incredibly low in the car and clamp the scissor door shut. Visibility in every direction, save dead ahead, is a joke. The 5.7-litre, 455-bhp engine bellows even at idle, and the five-speed gearbox feels like it has been designed for a truck. Every control is leaden and the car feels as wide as an office block and about as manoeuvrable.

In fact, unless you take the Countach by the scruff and drive it very hard indeed, it is a pretty unpleasant device. Put it to good and proper use, however, and it all starts to make startlingly good sense. As the speeds rise, the weight seems to leave the car with the steering becoming light and communicative in your hands as the rampant V12 hurls you down the road. You can dial up 160kph (100mph) on the speedometer with frightening ease.

Yet the Countach is not a malevolent car. It needs respect, certainly, a stern hand and a brave heart, but it is not a car waiting to slip a blade between your ribs at the first sign of a mistake.

It is, instead, a truly great car, and one that deserves to be taken rather more seriously than its joke looks suggest.

Its cabin was never going to be to everyone's taste, but it at least filled the needs of poseurs with ease. The driving position is not among the best and note the wind-up windows on this, once the most expensive supercar you could buy.

207

Lamborghini Countach QV

Manufactured: 1985-88
Number of cars: 610

Dimensions

Length: 4,140mm
Width: 2,000mm
Height: 1,070mm
Wheelbase: 2,450mm
Front track/rear track: 1,492mm/1,606mm
Kerb weight: 1,446kg

Engine

Capacity: 5,167cc
Bore/stroke: 86mm/75mm
Construction: Aluminium head,
    aluminium block
Valve gear: 4 valves per cylinder, dohc
Compression ratio: 9.5:1
Max power: 455bhp at 7,000rpm
Max torque: 369lb ft at 5,200rpm
Gearbox: 5-speed manual

Brakes

Front: Ventilated discs
Rear: Ventilated discs
Servo assistance/anti-lock: Yes/no

Suspension

Front: Double wishbones, coil springs,
    anti-roll bar
Rear: Double wishbones, coil springs,
    anti-roll bar

Steering system

Rack and pinion

Wheels and tyres

Wheel size: 8.5 x 15in (f), 12.0 x 15in (r)
Construction: Alloy
Tyre size: 225/50 VR 15 (f), 345/35 VR 15 (r)

Claimed performance

0-97kph (0-60mph): 4.9sec
Max speed: 286kph (178mph)

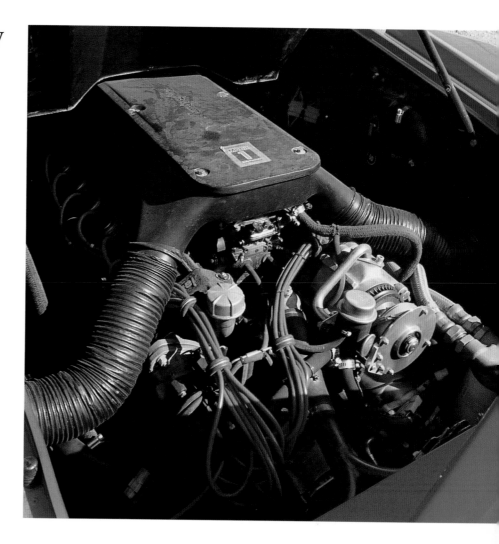

This 5.2-litre V12 sounds rather hotter than it looks.
Before the days of fuel injection or catalytic converters,
carburettors ruled the supercar world. The Countach
had six in total.

Lotus Elise

The Elise heralded a new dawn in sportscar handling, performance, eclipsing even the likes of the Caterham Seven. Its trick is to provide the feel and communication you need without any of the unwelcome kickback. On the limit of its performance, it is truly extraordinary.

Every so often a sportscar is designed that rises to the very summit of its class. On the one hand, it is not that an uncommon occurrence since cars do tend to improve as lessons are learned from previous generations of vehicles. It is, on the other hand, a rare and precious event when a new sportscar is produced that completely redefines the class in which it competes, rendering all predecessors instantly and obviously obsolete. Jaguar has done it twice – in 1948 with the XK120 and again in 1961 with the E-type – and now it is the turn of Lotus.

The Lotus Elise is remarkable for two reasons. The first is that its strengths are so overwhelming that its weaknesses, of which there are several, are completely overshadowed. The second is that Lotus, in the form of the Elise, has achieved that which so many other car manufacturers try for and fail – it has remained true to its traditions while looking into the future.

The Lotus tradition says that all that is good in a sportscar stems from minimizing the weight of the vehicle, and that its products should use innovation and the latest technological advances to achieve that single, overriding goal.

You can see its point. A light car will be quicker, more economical, better braked and swifter through the corners than an otherwise identically specified but heavier vehicle. To achieve this end, Lotus decided to build not only the Elise's body but also its underlying structure entirely from light-weight aluminium. In this respect it is rare, but not unique.

What, however, does make the little Lotus different to any other car on the road is that, believe it or not, the structure is not welded together, it is glued. This may sound horrific to those who are not aware of the latest advances in bonding technology but the result is not simply a car that carries just half the weight of a

family hatchback, but one that is also incredibly rigid and strong.

This is crucial, for it provided a hugely stable structure from which to derive the car's dynamic abilities. With this platform, and the unrivalled talents of its chassis engineers, Lotus has created what many authorities contend to be the finest handling sportscar the world has yet to see.

Remarkably, then, it is also a car in need of considerable improvement. Its basic 1.8-litre Rover engine may have twin overhead camshafts and 16 valves but it still feels more at home in a Rover hatch-

back than a Lotus sportscar, while the gearbox – an undistinguished, clunking five-speeder, has no place in such a car.

Even so, despite the serious and obvious faults that lie within the Elise, and they include a fiddly hood and the fact that it's undignified in the extreme to climb either in or out with it in place, it will rightly be remembered not simply as one of the finest Lotuses but also one of the greatest sportscars of our time. The lack of a bit more power and a really snappy six-speed transmission is now all that stand between it being one of the greatest of all time.

Elise cockpit is entirely focussed on the driver. There are no frills, just bare aluminium, a minimum of switches and stalks and nothing to interfere with your driving pleasure. Instruments are a mixture of analogue and LCD read-outs and work brilliantly well

Lotus Elise

Manufactured: 1996 (on-going)
Number of cars: 25,000 to date

Dimensions
Length: 3,726mm
Width: 1,820mm
Height: 1,202mm
Wheelbase: 2,300mm
Front track/rear track: 1,440mm/1,453mm
Kerb weight: 723kg

Engine
Capacity: 1,796cc
Bore/stroke: 100mm/79mm
Construction: Aluminium head,
    aluminium block
Valve gear: 4 valves per cylinder, dohc
Compression ratio: 10.5:1
Max power: 118bhp at 5,500rpm
Max torque: 122lb ft at 3,000rpm
Gearbox: 5-speed manual

Brakes
Front: Ventilated discs
Rear: Ventilated discs
Servo assistance/anti-lock: No/no

Suspension
Front: Double wishbones, coil springs,
    anti-roll bar
Rear: Double wishbones, coil springs,
    anti-roll bar

Steering system
Rack and pinion

Wheels and tyres
Wheel size: 5.5 x 15in (f), 6.0 x 16in (r)
Construction: Cast alloy
Tyre size: 185/55 VR 15 (f), 205/50 VR 16 (r)

Claimed performance
0-97kph (0-60mph): 5.5sec
Max speed: 200kph (124mph)

A Rover twin-cam four is a fine engine when installed in the front of a Rover hatchback, but it faces an altogether different challenge in the back of the Lotus Elise. While the engine provides adequate performance, it is not in any greater state of tune than when it came out the factory, and it lacks the gut-wrenching response the Elise needs to provide a complete dynamic picture. Rumours abound of a hot version, and even one with six cylinders being slotted into the Elise but, to date, none has been forthcoming.

BMW 3.0CSL

The BMW 3.0CSL is one of those cars that just grows on you for reasons that are not readily apparent at the time. In a book such as this, with so many ultimate achievers and superlative record breakers, it is a little odd at first to consider this BMW model among their number.

It was a special car for sure, building on the progress of the 3.0CS coupé whose bodywork it shared and living alongside the almost identical 3.0CSI. Indeed, apart from the identifying badge on the back of the car, slightly wider wheels and some compensating wheel-arch extensions, there was little way of telling one from the other unless you knew what to look for.

Yet the CSL became special to those who drove it in ways that could not be seen. It was, in fact, a device intended not simply as an everyday road coupé but, instead, a car to homologate one of the most famous racing BMWs of all time –

the wildly bewinged 'Batmobile'. This is why the 3.0CSL came into production complete with a carefully tuned and stretched 3-litre, six-cylinder engine, wider wheels and fatter tyres and, most crucially of all, an especially lightened body that utilized aluminium for the doors, bonnet and boot.

The result was BMW's finest car of the 1970s, and not just by a whisker but by a considerable margin. They created in the 3.0CSL a road-going automobile that combined the thrills of an especially constructed, highly tuned special with the everyday domestic dependability and excellence that underpinned BMW's formidable reputation.

And, of course, it was a beautiful car in a way that today's 850i coupé fails so clearly to understand. Its lines are ineffably right from bumper to bumper, proving not simply beautifully but also unmistakably a BMW.

Today, its performance seems modest with its 3-litre, 200-bhp engine pushing the sharp-fronted CSL through the air at no more than about 217kph (135mph), but in its day it was faster than all bar the swiftest of supercars yet it would swallow four adults and all their luggage in complete comfort.

The CSL's handling, too, defies those critics who say that BMWs from this era were handfuls that would rapidly lose control unless driven with the utmost care in the wet. Though the grip levels from its period tyres cannot in any way be compared with those achieved even by humble family saloons today, the CSL was a surprisingly faithful and rewarding car that hinted at the overall dynamic competence that would win the racing version so much silverware on the track.

As is often the case, it is only with the benefit of hindsight that we come to see what made the CSL one of the true greats of automotive history. It provided BMW with an identity and a reputation for building the best sports coupés. And, to this day, BMW has never looked back. Those of us who have enjoyed the M3s and M6s over years have the CSL to thank for them.

Not simply a beautiful shape but one that also shouts out its BMW heritage. The CSL's shark-like nose is inimitable and its sleek profile particularly successful.

BMW 3.0CSL

Manufactured: 1971-75
Number of cars: 1,039

Dimensions
Length: 4,648mm
Width: 1,676mm
Height: 1,371mm
Wheelbase: 2,311mm
Front track/rear track: 1,148mm/1,387mm
Kerb weight: 1,350kg

Engine
Capacity: 3,003cc
Bore/stroke: 83mm/87mm
Construction: Aluminium head,
  iron block
Valve gear: 2 valves per cylinder, sohc
Compression ratio: n/a
Max power: 200bhp at 5,500rpm
Max torque: n/a
Gearbox: 4-speed manual

Brakes
Front: Ventilated discs
Rear: Ventilated discs
Servo assistance/anti-lock: Yes/no

Suspension
Front: Struts, lower link, coil springs,
  anti-roll bar
Rear: Semi-trailing arms, coil springs,
  anti-roll bar

Steering system
Ball and nut

Wheels and tyres
Wheel size: 7.0 x 14in
Construction: Cast alloy
Tyre size: 195/70 VR 14

Claimed performance
0-97kph (0-60mph): 7.3sec
Max speed: 217kph (135mph)

This simple, single-cam straight-six engine was to work wonders under the bonnet of the 3.0CSL. It used fuel-injection, which was unusual in its day, but eschewed the increasingly popular five-speed gearbox in favour of an old-fashioned four-speeder.

Mercedes 300SL

The Mille Miglia, a 1,600-km (1,000-mile) race from Brescia in Northern Italy to Rome and back, was the finest road race the world has ever seen. It was won in 1955 by Stirling Moss driving a Mercedes-Benz 300SLR in a time that was never beaten. It was Moss's most famous win.

Less well known but perhaps just as significant was the car that came fifth that year. It was another Mercedes, a 300SL driven by John Fitch, which was no different to the model you could have bought, for a massive £4000, straight from your local Mercedes showroom.

The 300SL was truly remarkable and not simply for its point-to-point speed. It was innovative, bringing to the production car techniques and technologies that had been either the exclusive preserve of racing cars or were simply brand new. It was the first to feature a true space-frame chassis, a process where, instead of merely bolting a body onto a chassis, the body itself was an integral part of the structure of the car. It was for this reason rather than fashion that the 300SL was fitted with its legendary "gullwing" doors. Simply put, because there were substantial steel chassis tubes running down each side of the car, normal doors were out of the question. More significantly, it was the first production car to feature fuel injection, a means of introducing fuel to the engine employed by every new car design these days. It allowed the 3-litre, six cylinder engine to develop not simply huge amounts of power but also to continue to run reliably and indefinitely at maximum output.

The real magic of the 300SL was not simply its performance but the manner and ease with which it was provided. At the time there was a handful of technically road legal sports cars which might be able to keep up with it in a straight line but none which could approach the ease and

Mercedes 300SL

Manufactured: 1954-57
Number of cars: 1,400

Dimensions
Length: 4,673mm
Width: 1,778mm
Height: 1,295mm
Wheelbase: 2,388mm
Front track/rear track: 1,371mm/1,422mm
Kerb weight: 1,252kg

Engine
Capacity: 2,996cc
Bore/stroke: 85mm/88mm
Construction: Aluminium head,
    cast-iron block
Valve gear: 2 valves per cylinder, sohc
Compression ratio: 8.5:1
Max power: 240bhp at 6,100rpm
Max torque: 217lb ft at 4,800rpm
Gearbox: 4-speed manual

Brakes
Front: Drum
Rear: Drum
Servo assistance/anti-lock: Yes/no

Suspension
Front: Double wishbones, coil springs,
    anti-roll bar
Rear: Swing axles, coil springs

Steering system
Unassisted rack and pinion

Wheels and tyres
Wheel size: 6.5 x 15in
Construction: Pressed steel
Tyre size: 6.5 x 15 crossplies

Claimed performance
0-97kph (0-60mph): 8.8sec
Max speed: 210kph (135mph) plus

civility with which the gullwing would bowl you down the road. And while no standard car would quite exceed the magic 240kph (150mph) that has so often been suggested was within the car's capabilities without modification, any old SL would crack 233kph (145mph), a speed every bit as impressive as 321kph (200mph) today. The SL, however, was not perfect. Its rear suspension design meant the band between cornering with little apparent effort and losing control of the car was narrower than was perhaps wide for a road car but, that said, the speeds at which this limitation would appear were so far beyond the standards of the day that few ever found themselves in trouble as a result. For most, it was simply the most advanced road car that had ever been built.

Overleaf: The 300SL was a great looking car, made famous by the now legendary gullwing doors. Its shape worked well, too, helping it to speeds that were almost unheard of on the public roads of the mid-1950s.

The straight-six engine had early mechanical fuel injection. It was both strong and powerful.

Ferrari 288 GTO

In 1971, Ferrari produced the Berlinetta Boxer and claimed it would do 302kph (188mph). The only problem was that the Boxer was nothing like as swift. In favourable conditions, a good example might crack 273kph (170mph), just. So when Ferrari announced the 288GTO in 1984 and said that it, too, would do 302kph (188mph), it raised an eyebrow or two among the *cognoscenti*.

And then they drove it. This beautiful mid-engined sportscar may have looked like Ferrari's then junior supercar, the 308, but that was mere illusion, for this GTO, like its illustrious predecessor, was born from lessons learned on the track. This is why its twin-turbocharged, 2.8-litre V8 engine came straight from the Lancia LC2 sports-prototype, for which Ferrari had originally designed the engine, while the body was one of the first to be built from such complex composite materials as Kevlar and carbon fibre. In charge was Dr

Harvey Postlethwaite, who was seconded from designing Ferrari Formula One cars to oversee the construction of the GTO.

It was perhaps no surprise, then, to learn that the GTO was Ferrari's most serious road car to date as well as one of his most beautiful. Crucially, it was also the car that provided the basis from which the peerless F40 was developed. And it is that which, over the years, has proven to be the GTO's problem: with a kid-brother like that, coming out of its shadows was never going to be easy.

What people tend not, therefore, to realize about the GTO is not simply that it is a rather more rare car than the F40 (Ferrari built 272 as against 1,100 for the F40) but that it would still show a clean set of exhaust pipes to any road-going Ferrari made today – now that F50 production has ceased. With just 400bhp, it may not be quite as powerful as today's flagship, the 550 Maranello, but it is

Ferrari 288 GTO

Manufactured: 1984-85
Number of cars: 272

Dimensions
Length: 4,291mm
Width: 1,915mm
Height: 1,120mm
Wheelbase: 2,451mm
Front track/rear track: 1,560mm/1,562mm
Kerb weight: 1,160kg

Engine
Capacity: 2,855cc
Bore/stroke: 80mm/71mm
Construction: Alloy head, alloy block
Valve gear: 4 valves per cylinder, dohc
Compression ratio: 7.6:1
Max power: 400bhp at 7,000rpm
Max torque: 466lb ft at 3,800rpm
Gearbox: 5-speed manual

Brakes
Front: Ventilated discs
Rear: Ventilated discs
Servo assistance/anti-lock: Yes/no

Suspension
Front: Double wishbones, coil springs,
  anti-roll bar
Rear: Double wishbones, coil springs,
  anti-roll bar

Steering system
Unassisted rack and pinion

Wheels and tyres
Wheel size: 8.0 x 16in (f), 10.0 x 16in (r)
Construction: Cast alloy
Tyre size: 225/55 VR 16 (f), 255/50 VR 16 (r)

Claimed performance
0-97kph (0-60mph): 4.7sec
Max speed: 304kph (189mph)

rather small and, with all those clever materials, substantially lighter, too.

This means that a 288GTO will explode up the road given even the slightest chance, taxing your concentration to the limit just to keep up with the acceleration. Right on the limit it needs watching, since its chassis lacks the friendliness that Ferrari engineered into the F40, but to some this merely adds to the challenge.

It is not, however, the GTO's performance that is its most remarkable achievement; it is the fact that such speed is achieved in total comfort and civility. This makes it a wonderfully refined and effective intercontinental missile. Faster, more fun and more memorable though the F40 is, it was the GTO that proved massively more useable.

Unlike its F40 successor, the GTO cabin was meant to be comfortable over very long distances. Electric windows and full air conditioning were fitted as standard.

Porsche 928GT

It is hard to imagine any sportscar winning the Car of the Year award in these days of political correctness. If it does not swallow families whole and their luggage, sip fuel like tea at an English garden party and blow lavender-scented fresh air out of its exhaust, the jury tends not to be that interested. So it says something for the all-round appeal of the Porsche 928 that, back in 1978, it won this most coveted of awards.

Back then, it was the car designed to replace the 911, which, at 15 years old, had already lasted longer than just about any sportscar in history. But where the 911 was wild, the 928 was conventional, using a water-cooled engine in the nose instead of an air-cooled unit in the tail. Back then, it was thought to be viciously fast with its 240bhp V8 engine pushing it to the door of 257kph (160mph).

Porsche, on the other hand, thought differently and developed the 928 until, by the time it had become the 928GT, it sported 330bhp and a top speed a long way on the far side of 274kph (170mph). And, for a while, it occupied a niche in the market as the greatest all-round supercar of the lot. Thanks to Porsche's chassis wizards, it was a car that would not only cover ground and corner at phenomenally high speeds, but you could also hurl it around racetracks all day without it ever biting back or, unthinkably for a new Porsche, breaking.

But even this only goes halfway to explaining the 928GT magic. It was the fact that it would do all the above as well as behave like a long-distance limousine that made it appeal to certain sectors of the business community like no other car before or, some still maintain, since. And, like all Porsches, the 928s rarely, if ever, went wrong, with examples boasting 240,000km (150,000 miles) on their clocks feeling merely nicely run in.

Porsche 928GT

Manufactured: 1990-92
Number of cars: 2,924

Dimensions
Length: 4,520mm
Width: 1,836mm
Height: 1,282mm
Wheelbase: 2,500mm
Front track/rear track: 1,551mm/1,546mm
Kerb weight: 1,566kg

Engine
Capacity: 4,957cc
Bore/stroke: 100mm/79mm
Construction: Aluminium head,
    aluminium block
Valve gear: 4 valves per cylinder, dohc
Compression ratio: 10.1:1
Max power: 330bhp at 6,200rpm
Max torque: 317lb ft at 4,100rpm
Gearbox: 5-speed manual

Brakes
Front: Ventilated discs
Rear: Ventilated discs
Servo assistance/anti-lock: Yes/yes

Suspension
Front: Double wishbones, coil springs,
    anti-roll bar
Rear: Semi-trailing, coil springs,
    anti-roll bar

Steering system
Power-assisted rack and pinion

Wheels and tyres
Wheel size: 8.0 x 16in (f), 9.0 x 16in (r)
Construction: Cast alloy
Tyre size: 225/50 ZR 16 (f), 245/45 ZR 16 (r)

Claimed performance
0-97kph (0-60mph): 5.6sec
Max speed: 266kph (165mph)

In the end, this fine car was killed by the one assassin you would least expect of all. It was the 911, the car that the 928 had been sent to eliminate. The 911 refused to lie down when the 928 appeared and, once it had been refined into its current form, it boasted nearly all the civility of the 928 plus that traditionalist's slice of excitement the 928 would never quite capture. Porsche decided that it would stick by its old soldier and dispose of its now ageing lieutenant to make space for production of the Boxer, the new, 21st-century Porsche. Do not, however, perceive the 928 to have been anything less than a roaring success: not only was it the Car of the Year, it also survived for 18 years, which is more than most super-cars can claim.

This V8 engine started life with just 240bhp and two valves per cylinder. The GT version boasted a rather more meaningful 330bhp along with one of the most convincing V8 howls ever to come from under the bonnet of a European supercar.

Porsche 356 Speedster

You can see both the lines of the VW Beetle and the Porsche 911 in the outline of the Speedster. It was more fun than fast, even when new.

The saying 'If it looks right it is right' is dangerous at the best of times but there can be few areas in which such a sweeping generalization has been disproved than in the arena of the motor car. Its history is littered with great looking cars, from the 4-litre Bentley of 1931 to the McLaren F1 of 1994, which have proven to be financially disastrous to their makers.

The Porsche 356 Speedster might not have been an utter disaster, since it was never manufactured in sufficient quantities to do serious damage, but if you look back through Porsche's illustrious history, few indeed of their products have both looked so good and, commercially, have done so badly.

It was the Americans who, back in 1954, wanted the Speedster as a cheaper, faster version of the Cabriolet in which owners could both bask in the Californian sunshine and succeed in amateur racing.

The car Porsche produced was not simply fast and cheap, it was also one of the defining shapes of the 1950s, and one that did perhaps more than any other to stamp the glamour all over Porsche's name and gain it the reputation that it retains to this day. What is odd about the shape is that, at the time, some called it ugly and made unflattering references to an upturned bath on wheels. Today, it seems breathtakingly beautiful, a brilliant blend of scientific sculpting by the wind and minimalist design execution. Its lines are

226

Porsche 356 Speedster

Manufactured: 1953-55
Number of cars: 900

Dimensions
Length: 3,835mm
Width: 1,651mm
Height: 1,219mm
Wheelbase: 2,057mm
Front track/rear track: 1,295mm/1,245mm
Kerb weight: 815kg

Engine
Capacity: 1,582cc
Bore/stroke: 83mm/74mm
Construction: Alloy head, alloy block
Valve gear: 2 valves per cylinder, ohv
Compression ratio: 9.0:1
Max power: 75bhp at 5,000rpm
Max torque: 86lb ft at 3,700rpm
Gearbox: 4-speed manual

Brakes
Front: Drums
Rear: Drums
Servo assistance/anti-lock: No/no

Suspension
Front: Trailing arms, torsion bar
  springing
Rear: Swing axle, torsion bar springing

Steering system
Unassisted worm and peg

Wheels and tyres
Wheel size: 5.0 x 16in
Construction: Pressed steel
Tyre size: 5.0 x 16in

Claimed performance
0-97kph (0-60mph): 12sec
Max speed: 169kph (105mph)

among the cleanest and best integrated of any shape to take to the public road, while the details, such as the super-short windscreen and spartan interior, provided styling cues that Porsche was to use for another 40 years.

As a driving machine, the Speedster, like all 356s, provided an unlikely blend of simple pleasures followed by rather too much exciting entertainment if you pushed hard. Various engines were made available during the course of its life, from a humble, Beetle-derived 1.5-litre, pushrod motor to a race-bred, quad-cam unit pushing out 100bhp and giving the Speedster more than respectable performance.

Nevertheless, even the more modestly powered Speedsters needed watching when they were on the limit or if in the wet: the swing-axle rear suspension could cause the car to pitch into a spin with remarkably little warning, conferring a reputation on the handling of rear-engine Porsches that the marque to this day has had trouble shaking.

Then again, the Speedster was always at its best buzzing along in the sunshine where you could concentrate on soaking up its unlikely beauty and undoubted appeal. The greatest Porsche ever made it is not; the prettiest? Almost certainly.

The cabin is a typical example of German minimalist styling. All you need to drive the car is presented simply and elegantly, while everything else is omitted. It has a huge wheel, fashionable for the time, but not really essential. Thanks to its rear engine and light-weight construction, the Speedster required virtually no effort to drive.

BMW 2002 Turbo

Turbocharging is so common now it is taken for granted. The simple principle of using the exhaust gases to drive a pump to impel air under pressure back into the engine, hence increasing its charge density and giving the effect of an increased capacity, is used for all manner of reasons, not simply to provide extra power. Some manufacturers use turbos to make their engines quieter, others deploy the technique to create cleaner exhaust gases, while some even use turbos to promote fuel economy.

Back in 1974 it was not quite like this. Though the principle was well known and had been used in racing, it had not been possible to create a turbocharged engine with sufficiently docile manners to stand incorporation within a road car. Then BMW created the 2002 Turbo. So keen was the company to make sure that nobody failed to understand the significance of this, it wrote the word 'Turbo' in dazzling decals along both sides of the car, on the bootlid and even in mirror-image on the deep front spoiler.

Today we are used to turbos cutting in with a noticeable surge at little more than idling speed but, back then, BMW had yet to refine the art to so delicate a form. At first it was so slow you thought something was wrong with it; its acceleration would scarcely do justice to a 2-litre car without a turbocharger. But then, at 4,000rpm, it all happened at once. There is nothing remotely subtle about the way the 2002 Turbo delivers its power once it finally arrives: the whole lot is dropped in your lap in a single instant. If you are not taken entirely by surprise, you will be able to reach for another gear before the rev-counter hits 6,000rpm, and then this most bizarre show starts all over again.

It can all be monitored from a little dial on the dashboard which shows the turbo-boost. The first half of the dial is white,

BMW 2002 Turbo

Manufactured: 1973-74
Number of cars: 1,672

Dimensions
Length: 4,216mm
Width: 1,626mm
Height: 1,339mm
Wheelbase: 2,502mm
Front track/rear track: 1,371mm/1,346mm
Kerb weight: 1,103kg

Engine
Capacity: 1,990cc
Bore/stroke: 89mm/80mm
Construction: Alloy head, iron block
Valve gear: 2 valves per cylinder, sohc
Compression ratio: 6.9:1
Max power: 170bhp at 5,800rpm
Max torque: 117lb ft at 4,000rpm
Gearbox: 4-speed manual

Brakes
Front: Ventilated discs
Rear: Drums
Servo assistance/anti-lock: Yes/no

Suspension
Front: Struts, lower wishbones, coil springs,
anti-roll bar
Rear: Semi-trailing arms, coil springs,
anti-roll bar

Steering system
Worm and roller

Wheels and tyres
Wheel size: 5.5 x 13in
Construction: Pressed steel
Tyre size: 185/70 VR 13

Claimed performance
0-97kph (0-60mph): 7.3sec
Max speed: 209kph (130mph)

representing the part of the power band where the turbo makes no contribution; this is followed by a tiny flash of green where the mayhem breaks out. This is followed by a large streak of red representing an area of boost pressure into which you should not venture unless you enjoy writing cheques to have your engine rebuilt.

To be honest, the chassis was not quite up to it, though it did its best to keep all that power pointing in the right direction. In the end, though, the 2002 Turbo is not here because it was a good car – a claim it cannot credibly sustain – but more because it was a great car, one that not only provided a rare thrill at the time but also one that lit the path to the greatest performance-enhancing technological innovation of the late 20th century.

Germany's first turbo-charged production engine was not without its faults. Its power used to come in like somebody had thrown a switch but, when it was fully on song, nobody could quite believe a dowdy BMW saloon could behave in such an extra-ordinary fashion.

BMW Z1

It certainly was not its looks that made the Z1 a commercial failure. The drop-down doors were a brilliant touch, while the aggressive nose, smart alloys and ground-hugging purpose spoke of huge power. Sadly, that is all the Z1 did. For its chassis capabilities, it was woefully underpowered.

Given that BMW has some of the most able ranges of cars of any car manufacturer on the planet, it seems hard to think back to the Z1 and realize that it turned out to be one of the Bavarian marque's few bona fide failures of recent years.

What is a failure doing in this book? It is simple really – just because the Z1 failed to sell in sufficient numbers to ensure its survival does not mean for a moment that it was somehow a terrible car and, even then, as Ford GT40 fans will have read by now, that alone does not constitute grounds for exclusion from this book. In fact, the Z1 failed seriously on just two counts: its timing and its price.

Back at the end of the 1980s, the two-seat open sportscar was all but dead. Everyone knew it would eventually resurrect itself but nobody knew when and few were prepared even to stick a toe into the murky remains of this once buoyant market. When BMW tried and failed with the Z1, it merely warned everybody else to stay away for the next few years.

The sad thing about the Z1 was that it was a fine car and, with a little more power, it could have been a great one. Loosely based on the 3-series saloon, it used a 325i engine, directing power to the rear wheels through an innovative multi-link rear axle, which afforded suspension control never seen before on a BMW. With fine, shark-like styling and some inspired details, such as the doors that disappeared down into sills at the touch of a button, the Z1 promised all the thrills of open-air motoring with a full share of the confidence and pride of ownership that comes as standard with any BMW. Unfortunately, its chassis was almost too good, making the Z1 feel rather gutless. So while it would corner at almost bizarre speed, it lacked the surge once you were back on the straight.

BMW Z1

Manufactured: 1988-91
Number of cars: 8,000

Dimensions
Length: 3,924mm
Width: 1,702mm
Height: 1,244mm
Wheelbase: 2,438mm
Front track/rear track: 1,422mm/1,447mm
Kerb weight: 1,337kg

Engine
Capacity: 2,494cc
Bore/stroke: 84mm/75mm
Construction: Aluminium head,
   iron block
Valve gear: 2 valves per cylinder, sohc
Compression ratio: 8.8:1
Max power: 170bhp at 5,800rpm
Max torque: 164lb ft at 4,300rpm
Gearbox: 5-speed manual

Brakes
Front: Ventilated discs
Rear: Drums
Servo assistance/anti-lock: Yes/no

Suspension
Front: Struts, coil springs, anti-roll bar
Rear: Multi-link rear axle, coil springs,
   anti-roll bar

Steering system
Power-assisted rack and pinion

Wheels and tyres
Wheel size: 7.5 x 16in
Construction: Cast alloy
Tyre size: 225/45 ZR 16

Claimed performance
0-97kph (0-60mph): 7.9sec
Max speed: 219kph (136mph)

Even so, it might have survived on its looks and undoubted appeal if BMW had not decided to saddle it with so steep a price. In the UK, for example, it cost nearly £37,000 in 1989, or more than three times the price of a car such as the Peugeot 205GTI 1.9, which was not only more fun to drive, it was just as quick out of the blocks, too. And when an extra £7,000 on the price of a Z1 would buy a Porsche 911 Carrera 2 with true supercar performance and a top speed of 257kph (160mph), it is clear to see with hindsight that the Z1 was always going to struggle.

With just a little more patience and understanding, the BMW Z1 could still have been with us now. In the event, BMW realized its mistake, cut its losses and killed it off.

The Z1 had a great cabin that put together simple, traditional, BMW ergonomic values with great style and very funky seats, making the Z1 as good to drive on a long run as it looks. At speed, however, it was best to keep the doors up.

Jaguar XK8

Jaguar knows what it is like to suffer. After its halcyon days of the fifties and sixties, when both its road and race cars could seemingly do no wrong, it all started to go wrong in the seventies. The E-type was old and outdated and its replacement, the soft XJS, was a poor and ugly shadow of the act it attempted to follow. Jaguar was tossed about like a feather in the wind from independence to incorporation within the British Leyland Group (which was responsible for some of the worse-built cars ever to come out of Britain), back to independence, almost into the arms of General Motors and finally to ownership by Ford, who have it to this day.

When Ford's first act after taking over was to cancel the true E-type successor, the F-type, many pundits said that Jaguar would never survive, or that it would suffer the same fate that had befallen MG in the eighties.

They were wrong. Without Ford, we would never have had the XK8 and, without the XK8, Jaguar's global standing would be but a fraction of what it now is.

The XK8 is a brilliant car, the best to bear the badge since the original E-type. What is more, it's a clever car. Like the Aston Martin DB7 (which was evolved from the defunct F-type project when Ford took it away from Jaguar), there was not enough money or time to create an entirely new car, so the platform of the XJS would have to remain while all around it was changed.

You can still see the signs. Like the XJS, the XK8 is a large car with a surprisingly little amount of room inside, but in most other respects the comparison is insulting to the younger car. Just for a start, the XK8 has an all new V8 engine, designed entirely by Jaguar with only its sump-plug being common to anything wearing a Ford badge. It is one of the greatest engines

Jaguar XK8

Manufactured: 1996-2005
Number of cars: 76,000

Dimensions
Length: 4,760mm
Width: 2,015mm
Height: 1,296mm
Wheelbase: 2,588mm
Front track/rear track: 1,504mm/1,498mm
Kerb weight: 1,615kg

Engine
Capacity: 3,996cc
Bore/stroke: 86mm/86mm
Construction: Aluminium head,
    aluminium block
Valve gear: 4 valves per cylinder, dohc
Compression ratio: 10.8:1
Max power: 290bhp at 6,100rpm
Max torque: 290lb ft at 4,250rpm
Gearbox: 5-speed automatic

Brakes
Front: Ventilated discs
Rear: Ventilated discs
Servo assistance/anti-lock: Yes/yes

Suspension
Front: Double wishbones, coil springs,
    anti-roll bar
Rear: Lower wishbones, upper links,
    coil springs, anti-roll bar

Steering system
Power-assisted rack and pinion

Wheels and tyres
Wheel size: 8.0 x 17in
Construction: Cast alloy
Tyre size: 245/50 ZR 17

Claimed performance
0-97kph (0-60mph): 6.4sec
Max speed: 250kph (155mph)

made today, proving gutsy, powerful yet sufficiently refined to save the harmless Jaguar's reputation for hushed progress.

It also handles and rides unfathomably well thanks to suspension firm enough to keep total control in corners yet sufficiently well damped to iron out to nothing almost all imperfections in the road.

Most importantly of all, the XK8 is a fine looking car; not so jaw-slackeningly attractive as the E-type perhaps, but still a world away from the buttressed XJS.

In all the crucial areas of dynamic and static achievement, the XK8 scores higher than any road car with a cat on its nose, save the XJ220, and it is because of this that it is selling out all over the world. Long may it continue. Its every success will be deserved.

The XK8 interior is less pleasing than the outside. The driving position reveals the limitations of the XJS-derived platform and has inadequate legroom for tall drivers. The instruments are misguided as well, proving too faint and self-consciously recessed to work really well. Its five-speed automatic gearbox, on the other hand, is a delight.

Aston Martin V8 Zagato

It looked like a pig and went like a rocket. Few cars in Aston's chequered history courted controversy quite like the Zagato, but nobody ever accused it of failing to provide Aston-like performance. Until the current Vantage was made in 1994, it was the fastest, most powerful Aston ever produced.

Oddly, for such an irredeemably ugly car, had the Aston Martin V8 Zagato looked rather better, let's say it was just bland, it would probably have failed to make it into this book. In the event, so brilliantly, cataclysmically and appallingly ugly did it prove to be that its place in any history of outstanding cars would seem assured.

It was also, of course, really rather fast. Aston Martin only commissioned the Italian coachbuilders, Zagato, to build the coupés, though some convertibles sneaked out afterwards. In the mid-eighties era, when the concept of the ultra-fast, ultra-exclusive supercar was being pioneered by the likes of the Porsche 959 and Ferrari

288GTO, it was indeed a bold project on which to embark.

But Aston Martin timed it right and, despite the fact the Zagato proved to be neither as quick as the Porsche or Ferrari nor, indeed, as swift as the boffins at Aston Martin themselves had hoped, this did not stop them selling every one of these brutish missiles.

The starting point was the established and coveted V8 Vantage, a 400-bhp power house that looked great, sounded even better and was the fastest front-engined car in production at the time. The Zagato's brief was for a lighter, more powerful and aerodynamically efficient Vantage. Top-speed talk started at 320kph (200mph),

Aston Martin V8 Zagato

Manufactured: 1986-88
Number of cars: 52

Dimensions
Length: 4,390mm
Width: 1,860mm
Height: 1,295mm
Wheelbase: 2,610mm
Front track/rear track: 1,520mm/1,540mm
Kerb weight: 1,235kg

Engine
Capacity: 5,340cc
Bore/stroke: 100mm/85mm
Construction: Alloy head, alloy block
Valve gear: 2 valves per cylinder, dohc
Compression ratio: 9.3:1
Max power: 432bhp at 6,200rpm
Max torque: 390lb ft at 5,000rpm
Gearbox: 5-speed manual

Brakes
Front: Ventilated discs
Rear: Ventilated discs
Servo assistance/anti-lock: Yes/no

Suspension
Front: Double wishbones, coil springs,
  anti-roll bar
Rear: De Dion rear axle, coil springs,
  anti-roll bar

Steering system
Power-assisted rack and pinion

Wheels and tyres
Wheel size: 8.5 x 16in
Construction: Cast alloy
Tyre size: 255/50 VR 16

Claimed performance
0-97kph (0-60mph): 4.8sec
Max speed: 300kph (186mph)

though this was soon reined back to 300kph (186mph). A prototype came extremely close to this mark, but by the time the production models started to appear, a top end of 282kph (175mph) was rather more likely.

Even so, the Zagato still feels fast as its 5.3-litre, V8 motor pumps 432bhp through the rear wheels. It sounds wonderful too, with the deep throbbing of a large-capacity American motor overlaid by the sharp howl of an English racer.

The Zagato's life was short – spanning a few months between 1986 and 88 – but glorious. Today they are an increasingly rare sight as their values once more nudge northwards. Aston Martin only made 50, though. Looking at it now, it's a wonder it ever made it off the drawing board.

The classic English interior came complete with Smiths instruments, more leather and wood than you could imagine, and a slow and heavy gearbox. Ergonomically it is not a hard car to fault but, for striking the right blend of elegance and purpose, it worked better than the outside ever could.

TVR Cerbera

Essentially an elongated Chimaera with a roof, the Cerbera is not one of TVR's prettiest products, like the gorgeous Griffith. It is, however, without doubt not just TVR's quickest but also one of the fastest road cars ever to grace the public road.

Throughout the century-old history of the sportscar, many manufacturers have ruined their reputations by trying to be that little bit too clever and branching out into building machines other than those on which their reputations rested.

Few firms stand better able to deny this failing than TVR. Half a century ago TVR was building simple, strong sportscars, which more than made up for in power what they lacked in sophistication. Today it is exactly the same, and it is this focus that has ensured the survival of Britain's largest independent car company.

Its flagship is the Cerbera, and if it sounds like the sister of the dog that guarded the gates of hell, that is nothing compared to what it is like to drive. While remaining true to its TVR tradition, the Cerbera breaks with recent TVR history in that not only is it a closed coupé with tiny rear seats, but it also comes powered by

TVR's own engine, not a unit bought in from a major manufacturer.

To the unsuspecting, the results are absolutely terrifying. For the same price as an executive saloon, the Cerbera provides performance to embarrass almost every supercar on the streets, requiring, at the very least, a new Porsche 911 Turbo before you will find another that will even stand a chance of keeping up. And it is not simply a short, sharp shock – find the space and the Cerbera will take you past 290kph (180mph) in less time than you could conceive.

Why, then, are we not hailing the Cerbera as one of the greatest cars of all time, one that brings to the 1990s the same ground-breaking value that the Jaguar E-type did to the 1960s? There are two essential reasons. The first is snob value. By the time the E-type was born, its makers had already won Le Mans five times and its car was one of the most

TVR Cerbera

Manufactured: 1996 (on-going)
Number of cars: 2,100 to date

Dimensions

Length: 4,280mm
Width: 1,865mm
Height: 1,220mm
Wheelbase: 2,566mm
Front track/rear track: 1,464mm/1,470mm
Kerb weight: 1,177kg

Engine

Capacity: 4,185cc
Bore/stroke: 88mm/86mm
Construction: Aluminium head,
   aluminium block
Valve gear: 2 valves per cylinder, sohc
Compression ratio: 10.5:1
Max power: 350bhp at 6,500rpm
Max torque: 320lb ft at 6,500rpm
Gearbox: 5-speed manual

Brakes

Front: Ventilated discs
Rear: Ventilated discs
Servo assistance/anti-lock: Yes/no

Suspension

Front: Double wishbones, coil springs,
   anti-roll bar
Rear: Double wishbones, coil springs,
   anti-roll bar

Steering system

Rack and pinion

Wheels and tyres

Wheel size: 7.5 x 16in
Construction: Cast alloy
Tyre size: 225/45 ZR 16 (f), 235/50 ZR 16 (r)

Claimed performance

0-97kph (0-60mph): 4sec
Max speed: 298kph (185mph)

beautiful shapes ever seen. TVR has yet to seriously prove itself in competition against other manufacturers, and the Cerbera – while pleasant on the eye – is not the most graceful shape on the road. Second, despite a baffling array of electronic tricks and gizmos, the Cerbera is still dynamically a little crude, with handling that, while capable of looking after the power, does little to inspire confidence in the driver in the way that those others capable of accelerating so hard achieve.

Even so, we should be happy to have the Cerbera. There are perhaps only half a dozen cars in this book with even a hope of matching the TVR's shattering performance, and none at all that will provide room for four people on board.

Its bizarre interior works remarkably well and shows real flair and innovation. The dials are truly beautiful and all functions are available without taking your hands off the steering wheel. The novel fresh air vent works well, too.

Lister Storm

In the 1950s, by using a combination of a talented designer, sound business sense and an extraordinary driver, Brian Lister was able to create a racing car company that, often as not, humbled the biggest names in the sport, from Ferrari to Aston Martin and Jaguar. Tragically the driver, the fearfully disabled Archie Scott-Brown, was killed during a race in 1958. The next year, Lister closed its doors.

Its name, however, lives on, with Brian Lister's approval, and Lister Cars is now producing both road and racing versions of its Storm supercar.

The Storm is not for those with nervous dispositions. The looks alone are enough to induce shock. And behind this brutal façade lies nothing at all to suggest this wolf has the heart of a sheep. On the contrary, the Storm's heart is a Jaguar V12 motor, stretched to seven litres and with two superchargers to create something in the region of 600bhp.

This is not the Storm's greatest achievement. Cars such as the Storm, which are created by hand in numbers that make Aston Martin look like General Motors, are often seriously flawed as their creators lack the resources to develop properly all the ancillary systems, which have usually been bought in. Not the Storm. Not only will it do 322kph (200mph), it will do it with civility and, rather more impressively and importantly, total stability. That aerodynamic shape may not be pretty, but it certainly does its job well.

It has its flaws, as all such cars do. It feels cumbersome when not on open roads and it is tricky to drive through town not simply because its gearbox is heavy but also because the clutch is appallingly stiff. It also tends to kick and bump over imperfections in the road surface more than many supercars might.

Yet this does not detract from Lister's essential achievement. With tiny resources

Lister Storm

Manufactured: 1993–2004
Number of cars: 25

Dimensions
Length: 4,547mm
Width: 1,976mm
Height: 1,321mm
Wheelbase: 2,591mm
Front track/rear track: 1,867mm/1,930mm
Kerb weight: 1,664kg

Engine
Capacity: 6,997cc
Bore/stroke: 94mm/84mm
Construction: Alloy head, alloy block
Valve gear: 2 valves per cylinder, sohc
Compression ratio: 10.5:1
Max power: 594bhp at 6,100rpm
Max torque: 580lb ft at 3,450rpm
Gearbox: 6-speed manual

Brakes
Front: Ventilated discs
Rear: Ventilated discs
Servo assistance/anti-lock: Yes/no

Suspension
Front: Double wishbones, coil springs,
  anti-roll bar
Rear: Double wishbones, coil springs,
  anti-roll bar

Steering system
Power-assisted rack and pinion

Wheels and tyres
Wheel size: 9.5 x 18in (f), 12.0 x 18in (r)
Construction: Cast alloy
Tyre size: 245/40 ZR 18 (f), 325/30 ZR 18 (r)

Claimed performance
0-97kph (0-60mph): 4.7sec
Max speed: 322kph (200mph)

it has created a supercar as effective as it is outlandish and one that, despite its mighty cost, will always appeal to the rich looking for a truly unique example of a British supercar with a badge on the front proud enough to rival any others. The Storm works well on the track too, regularly outpacing racing cars from the likes of Porsche, despite the perceived disadvantage of having an engine in front.

Best of all, however, is that the Storm remains true to the man whose name it proudly carries. Brian Lister only ever built powerful, front-engined, rear-wheel-drive sportscars and you can only imagine what the heroic Scott-Brown would have made of the Storm had he lived. The inevitable conclusion to which you are led is that he would have loved it.

The Storm's interior is truly superb considering it comes from such a small company. Its quality is among the best, with proper heating and ventilation, and with much attention being paid to sealing and overall refinement.

Jaguar XKSS

While not quite as beautiful as the D-type, on which it is so clearly based, the XKSS is still a truly gorgeous car. The wraparound windscreen smacks at some form of practicality but, in truth, it was still very much a race-track refugee.

There are very few cars in the world that truly deserve the name 'Racing Car for the Road'. Yet, over the years, many less than entirely scrupulous manufacturers have described or allowed their cars to be described with such a glowing term. Usually all it means is that its performance is slightly better than experience suggests for the class.

Yet of all the things that you could have called the Jaguar XKSS during its short and ultimately tragic life, it is 'Racing Car for the Road' that does it most justice.

For the XKSS was a D-type Jaguar, of the type that won the Le Mans 24-hour race three times on the trot, wearing just a smattering of addenda to make it a sensible proposition on the road as well as race track. Its bodywork was derived from the short-nosed D-type and featured a wraparound windscreen with wipers and a hood for those who found the D-type's perspex visor a little limiting.

Thereafter, it was pure D-type, from its suspension to its steering and brakes. And, of course, the magnificent engine came straight from the racing car, too. Displacing just 3.4-litres, the twin-cam six-cylinder motor not only pushed out 260bhp (which would be a remarkable enough figure even today) but it also displayed such a mild-mannered nature that should you want to take it to do the shopping it would be meek and good-tempered all the way there and back again.

It was, however, perhaps rather more likely that any XKSS owner would take it by the scruff and drive it like the thinly disguised racer it was. And when treated properly, the XKSS lost no time in proving it was the fastest car yet seen on the public road. There never was an official top-speed run conducted on the car, but the fact that the D-types would run at 290kph (180mph) at Le Mans would suggest that a top speed of perhaps 266kph

Jaguar XKSS

Manufactured: 1957
Number of cars: 16

Dimensions

Length: 4,267mm
Width: 1,676mm
Height: n/a
Wheelbase: 2,311mm
Front track/rear track: n/a
Kerb weight: 1,050kg

Engine

Capacity: 3,442cc
Bore/stroke: 83mm/106mm
Construction: Aluminium head,
    iron block
Valve gear: 2 valves per cylinder, dohc
Compression ratio: n/a
Max power: 260bhp at 6,000rpm
Max torque: n/a
Gearbox: 4-speed manual

Brakes

Front: Plain discs
Rear: Plain discs
Servo assistance/anti-lock: No/no

Suspension

Front: Double wishbones, torsion bar
    springs, anti-roll bar
Rear: Live rear axle, trailing arms, torsion
    bar springs, anti-roll bar

Steering system

Rack and pinion

Wheels and tyres

Wheel size: 6.5 x 16in
Construction: Pressed steel
Tyre size: 6.5 x 16in

Claimed performance

0-97kph (0-60mph): 5.5sec
Max speed: 225kph (140mph)

(165mph) from the XKSS's slightly less aerodynamic form was by no means out of the question.

And, because it was a racing Jaguar, its excellence did not stop at the engine. It handled beautifully, too, allowing perfectly controlled power-slides at over 160kph (100mph), while its brakes, like those of the D-type, were powerful discs and more than capable of dealing with the speed.

You might wonder, then, why the XKSS is a largely forgotten Jaguar, particularly as it was faster and better bred than the world-famous E-type, which it pre-dated by four years. The answer is simple and sad. One black day in 1957, fire swept through the factory where it was made, destroying everything in its path. Just 16 had been made.

The XKSS's typically Jaguar interior boasts a wonderfully detailed steering wheel and big instruments. Its horizontal gear-lever looks a little odd but the gearbox, like the car in general, is very easy to handle.

Aston Martin DB2/4 MkIII

The DB2/4 MkIII was the last of the truly bespoke Astons. It was replaced by the DB4, which, while much faster and a superb car in its own right, was more of a Grand Tourer than an all-out sportscar.

This is the unknown Aston Martin and, in all probability, the most underrated car ever produced by the marque. It was made in tiny numbers and it was the last of a breed of Astons we would ever see.

Though built between 1957 and 1959, its design was old even when new, using an Aston Martin chassis first seen in 1940 and an engine WO Bentley designed for Lagonda during the war, albeit heavily tuned and modified.

The DB2/4 MkIII was the ultimate development of the DB2, the '4' denoting its number of seats. By 1957 this, the world's first hatchback, was using a 3-litre twin-cam engine developing up to 178bhp

with special exhausts giving a top speed of around 201kph (125mph). This may not sound like much today and, even then, it was not much faster than the cheaper opposition from Jaguar, but, like all things Aston Martin, it was the manner in which its performance was achieved, not its sheer quantity, that counted.

Sitting on board with the huge, wood-rimmed steering wheel in your hands, listening to the glorious howl of the engine, you become aware of a sense of rare privilege, that you are sitting in a car that defines the art of English craftsmanship from the beautiful leather upholstery to the hand-beaten aluminium bodywork. All the controls, from the switchgear to

Aston Martin DB2/4

Manufactured: 1957-59

Number of cars: 551

Dimensions
Length: 4,356mm
Width: 1,651mm
Height: 1,359mm
Wheelbase: 2,515mm
Front track/rear track: 1,372mm/1,372mm
Kerb weight: 1,338kg

Engine
Capacity: 2,922cc
Bore/stroke: 83mm/90mm
Construction: Iron head, iron block
Valve gear: 2 valves per cylinder, dohc
Compression ratio: 8.2:1
Max power: 162bhp at 5,500rpm
Max torque: 180lb ft at 4,000rpm
Gearbox: 4-speed manual

Brakes
Front: Plain discs
Rear: Drums
Servo assistance/anti-lock: Yes/no

Suspension
Front: Trailing arms, coil springs,
   anti-roll bar
Rear: Live axle, parallel radius arms,
   coil springs

Steering system
Unassisted recirculating ball

Wheels and tyres
Wheel size: 6.0 x 16in
Construction: Steel, spoked
Tyre size: 6.0 x 16in

Claimed performance
0-97kph (0-60mph): 9.3sec
Max speed: 193kph (120mph)

the gear lever, operate with the same heavy precision, exuding a sense of quality.

It is also a beautiful car and, in this respect as well as in many others, it has the advantage over the other DB2s that preceded it. It may lack the flashy ostentation of the later DBs, but they, just as surely, lack its subtle prettiness.

These later cars also tend not to handle as well, being built to be capable chiefly on long touring trips. The MkIII, however, is not like this and feels like a stiff little sportscar by comparison, with much sharper reactions and more agility being provided at the expense of long-distance comfort. In this particular respect it fails even to come close to those that purported to succeed it.

The DB2/4 MkIII was easily the most beautiful of the road Astons produced at the Feltham factory after the Second World War. However, by 1957, when it was produced, its design was already old, based, as it was, on a chassis that first ran in 1940 and an engine designed during the war.

Dodge Charger

Unlikely as it may seem, this is one form of car heaven – driving a Charger like a rally car. With so much power and so little road grip, the car tends to slide about a bit at the best of times. Put it on a loose surface, however, and it will slither sideways with just the slightest provocation.

The American muscle-car is every bit as great an institution as the Italian supercar and, in its heyday, in the late 1960s before the oil crisis and legislation curtailed its activities, some of the most enigmatic cars of all were churned out of Detroit factories, ready to tear up the open road.

One of the most famous, fastest and best of these was the Dodge Charger. Any number of engines could be fitted behind its blind-eyed grille, but the biggest was the 7.2-litre V8 motor called the 'Magnum' for reasons that became immediately and abundantly clear the moment anyone fired one up.

Sophisticated it might not have been, improbably fast it undoubtedly was. Whether fitted with a three-speed automatic gearbox or a four-speed manual, it would leave black lines on the road whenever its driver chose, thanks to the handy

375bhp living underneath the bonnet complete with enough torque to topple skyscrapers. In a straight-line, 400-m (1312-ft) dash between a Charger and a Porsche 928, it would be America that would go home with the prize.

Certainly, the Europeans could run rings around it through the corners. Chargers are heavy, have simple suspension and a long wheelbase, none of which exactly promotes agility, but, even so, the Dodge manages to charm. It's all in the steering, which is impressively ghastly. Those used to driving European cars will not figure how the Americans coped with steering that only plots a suggested route through a corner. You can either let it find its own way around or constantly fine tune the wheel until you are pointing approximately where you want. Either way, the experience is one you are unlikely to forget.

Dodge Charger

Manufactured: 1968-69
Number of cars: 20,100

Dimensions

Length: 5,280mm
Width: 1,948mm
Height: 1,359mm
Wheelbase: 2,972mm
Front track/rear track: 1,511mm/1,504mm
Kerb weight: 1,689kg

Engine

Capacity: 7,219cc
Bore/stroke: 110mm/95mm
Construction: Cast-iron head,
   cast-iron block
Valve gear: 2 valves per cylinder, ohv
Compression ratio: 10.0:1
Max power: 375bhp at 4,000rpm
Max torque: 480lb ft at 3,200rpm
Gearbox: 3-speed automatic

Brakes

Front: Plain discs
Rear: Drums
Servo assistance/anti-lock: Yes/no

Suspension

Front: Upper and lower control arms,
   coil springs, anti-roll bar
Rear: Live axle, semi-elliptic leaf springs

Steering system

Power-assisted recirculating ball

Wheels and tyres

Wheel size: 5.5 x 15in
Construction: Pressed steel
Tyre size: 8.25 x 15in

Claimed performance

0-97kph (0-60mph): 6sec
Max speed: 209kph (130mph)

To be honest, a Charger does not make much sense in a European context. For a start, space is too confined and then there is the traffic, which is too congested for its mighty bulk and colossal dimensions to work well. But in its native land, where there is all the space a Charger could need, lots of straight lines and not too many corners, it is in its element. The low fuel prices, which make its gas-guzzling consumption a viable financial proposition, help, too. Out there, a form of

The monster Magnum V8 was the largest, if not quite the most powerful, engine Dodge fitted to the Charger. It became the car that defined the muscle-car breed that roamed North America in the late 1960s, that is until the oil crisis killed them off – though, as the Viper proves, not for ever.

motoring bliss can be achieved in the most unlikely scenarios, cruising across the open savannah, local radio stations abandoned in favour of the musical rumblings of the mighty Magnum, alone in America with only a 1969 Dodge Charger, the ultimate affordable muscle-car, for company.

Renault Five Turbo One

The original mid-engined Renault Five Turbo was never called 'Turbo One', but it is universally referred to that way today in order to distinguish it from the similar, but mass-produced, Turbo Two, that followed.

Imagine discovering that your grandmother was an assassin or that the local poodle filled the small hours of darkness terrorising rottweilers. The look on your face would not be dissimilar to that which appeared on the collective face of the world's press when Renault unveiled the mid-engined Renault Five Turbo. Called the Turbo One today (but not at the time), you would not have been more surprised had Rolls-Royce announced it was to build a Formula One Grand Prix racing car.

There was a certain method behind the madness of turning an inoffensive shopping trolley like the Five into one of the scariest devices ever to venture out on to the public road, but that is not what the world saw. It saw a mid-engined two-seater with a tiny but sky-high-tuned engine and a look so low and wide it appeared to have been squashed. And then they saw the Renault badge.

To Renault, it all made perfect sense. It needed a rally car and the rules dictated that it had to be based on a road car. The Five already had the engine and gearbox in front of the driver powering the front wheels so it was relatively straightforward to take the entire assembly, place it behind the driver, where the back seats once were, and direct the power through the rear-wheels, transforming a front-engined hatch into a mid-engined supercar at a stroke. Nor was the result some crude, special-stage refugee. It came specially

Renault Five Turbo One

Manufactured: 1980-82
Number of cars: 1,820

Dimensions

Length: 3,664mm
Width: 1,752mm
Height: 1,323mm
Wheelbase: 2,430mm
Front track/rear track: 1,346mm/1,474mm
Kerb weight: 940kg

Engine

Capacity: 1,397cc
Bore/stroke: 76mm/77mm
Construction: Iron head, iron block
Valve gear: 2 valves per cylinder, ohv
Compression ratio: 7.0:1
Max power: 160bhp at 6,000rpm
Max torque: 160lb ft at 3,250rpm
Gearbox: 5-speed manual

Brakes

Front: Plain discs
Rear: Plain discs
Servo assistance/anti-lock: Yes/no

Suspension

Front: Double wishbones, torsion bar
   springing, anti-roll bar
Rear: Double wishbones, coil springs,
   anti-roll bar

Steering system

Unassisted rack and pinion

Wheels and tyres

Wheel size: 5.5 x 14in (f), 7.5 x 14in (r)
Construction: Cast alloy
Tyre size: 190/55 VR 14 (f), 220/55 VR 14 (r)

Claimed performance

0-97kph (0-60mph): 7.7sec
Max speed: 201kph (125mph)

trimmed in lurid colours with banks of unique instruments to give a truly bespoke feel.

Those who drove it for the first time always set off wondering what all the fuss was about. After all, it only had an old, 1.4-litre pushrod engine with no sporting pretensions at all, and the acceleration seemed modest to say the least. They would think that right up to the first time the rev-counter needle went beyond 4,000rpm. All the warning you received was a whoosh as the turbo kicked in and threw the little Renault at the horizon. The engine might have been small, old and homespun, but it also happened to be incredibly strong. So all Renault had to do was force more and more turbo boost pressure on it until it came up with enough power – which, in rallying form, was around 300bhp from just 1.4-litres.

The engine was not the only scary component either – the chassis, with its wide track and tiny wheelbase used to twitch so much that it made the Porsche 911 of the day look well behaved. Even so, with a skilled driver in the right conditions, it would provide rewards beyond anything you would ever credit to a car wearing a Renault Five badge.

It may not look like much, but its tiny, pushrod 1.4-litre motor could be made to pack a punch bigger than almost anyone at the time imagined possible. It could be tuned to provide a reliable 200 horsepower for the road.

AC Cobra

Neither the most subtle nor the best car on the road, the Cobra relied on shock tactics to grab your attention, and then not let go. Back in the mid-1960s, testers had never seen or driven anything quite like it.

In 1964, an AC Cobra was driven along the M1 motorway at 298kph (185mph) as part of an entirely standard test prior to it competing at Le Mans. There was nothing illegal in the action and its driver thought nothing more about the event until he saw it splashed all over the newspapers. It became the singlemost oft quoted cause for the introduction of speed limits in the UK.

The Cobra, you will have gathered, was fast and even the road-going cars, with open bodywork rather than the closed coupé that hurtled down the M4, were far and away the quickest cars on the roads of the day. In 1965, *Autocar* magazine was among the first to define how swift the Cobra was by recording a 0-97kph (0-60mph) time of 5.5 seconds and a standing quarter-mile time of 13.9 seconds, both eclipsing anything the staff members of the magazine had known.

The Cobra started life as the AC Ace, a beautiful and quintessentially British sportster powered by a 2-litre, six-cylinder engine. Fine to drive though it was, it was not exactly the fastest thing on wheels until the Texan racing driver Caroll Shelby had the idea of replacing the delicate aluminium six with eight cylinders of finest Detroit iron. With a 4.7-litre capacity from the huge Ford engine, producing an even 300bhp, the Cobra created enough noise and power to claim, without fear of contradiction, to be the most exciting sportscar of its era.

It wasn't, however, exactly sophisticated. Though its suspension was improved over the years, it was always a car best to be savoured in a straight line as its handling lacked the fluency of some of the European supercars that came to rival it over time.

Perhaps the most remarkable characteristic of the Cobra was not, in fact, its speed, but its longevity. It has been in more or less continuous production since 1962 and, as AC Cars has been tossed from one financial crisis to another, the

AC Cobra

Manufactured: n/a
Number of cars: n/a

Dimensions
Length: 4,013mm
Width: 1,600mm
Height: 1,219mm
Wheelbase: 2,286mm
Front track/rear track: 1,359mm/1,410mm
Kerb weight: n/a

Engine
Capacity: 4,727cc
Bore/stroke: 102mm/73mm
Construction: Iron block, iron head
Valve gear: 2 valves per cylinder, ohv
Compression ratio: n/a
Max power: 300bhp at 5,750rpm
Max torque: 285lb ft at 4,500rpm
Gearbox: 4-speed manual

Brakes
Front: Plain discs
Rear: Plain discs
Servo assistance/anti-lock: Yes/no

Suspension
Front: Wishbones, transverse leaf springs,
　　anti-roll bar
Rear: Wishbones, transverse leaf springs,
　　anti-roll bar

Steering system
Rack and pinion

Wheels and tyres
Wheel size: 5.0 x 15in
Construction: Cast alloy

Claimed performance
0-97kph (0-60mph): 5.5sec
Max speed: 225kph (140mph)

fact that there is still global demand for this now distinctly expensive and ageing blockbuster has ensured the survival of Britain's oldest car marque.

Not only has the Cobra done this, it has also provided the inspiration for thousands of imitations. The Cobra must be the most copied car of all time, with some people building loving replicas with the correct engines and hand-beaten aluminium chassis, while others have been content to fashion an approximate shape from glass-fibre, install a humble engine and hope the looks alone will fool people into believing it is the real thing. In fact, if you see a Cobra shape rumbling along the road, do not be fooled as it is almost certain to be a fake. Many more imitations now exist than the glorious originals.

Cobras ranged in engine size and power from a fairly fruity 4.7-litre model to a knee-knocking 7-litre version, such as that pictured below. Really hot Cobras had 400bhp in road-tuned form. Closed coupés reached 298kph (185mph) with ease.

Alfa-Romeo
Montreal

The Alfa-Romeo Montreal should have been one of the greatest cars of our time. It should have been close to the top of the order in this book instead of languishing nearer the bottom. It should have been a wild success and brought back, at last, to Alfa-Romeo the kudos and respect stolen from it by Ferrari following the end of the war. Sadly, that is not how it happened.

The Montreal's body started life as a showcar, a glamorous styling exercise shown at the 1967 Expo in the Canadian city whose name it bore. Alfa-Romeo sales, while buoyant in Europe at the time, were slack to say the least in all of North America, and its mission was to add some glitz to the name of this proud firm. It was well received – indeed so popular did its

beautiful shape prove that Alfa-Romeo decided to put it into production. Its only problem was finding a V8 engine for it, the only type to power a credible sportscar in the New World. The only V8 that Alfa owned lived in the back of its Tipo 33 sports-racing car. Undeterred, Alfa borrowed the engine and all its ancillaries, from its mechanical fuel-injection system to its five-speed gearbox, and bolted them under the nose of the Montreal.

One of the great shapes of all time now boasted one of the finest engines. It should have become an overnight classic.

Sadly, that is not how it happened. Alfa-Romeo, of all companies, should have known that there is more to a sportscar than its engine and appearance but, in too many areas, the Montreal proved to be

Alfa-Romeo Montreal

Manufactured: 1971-75
Number of cars: 3,925

Dimensions

Length: 4,216mm
Width: 1,671mm
Height: 1,240 mm
Wheelbase: 2,350mm
Front track/rear track: 1,379mm/1,341mm
Kerb weight: 1,276kg

Engine

Capacity: 2,593cc
Bore/stroke: 80mm/65mm
Construction: Aluminium head,
    aluminium block
Valve gear: 2 valves per cylinder, dohc
Compression ratio: 9.0:1
Max power: 200bhp at 6,500rpm
Max torque: 174lb ft at 4,750rpm
Gearbox: 5-speed manual

Brakes

Front: Ventilated discs
Rear: Ventilated discs
Servo assistance/anti-lock: Yes/no

Suspension

Front: Double wishbones, coil springs,
    anti-roll bar
Rear: Live axle, trailing arms, coil springs,
    anti-roll bar

Steering system

Recirculating ball

Wheels and tyres

Wheel size: 7.0 x 14in
Construction: Cast alloy
Tyre size: 195/70 VR 14

Claimed performance

0-97kph (0-60mph): 7.6sec
Max speed: 220kph (137mph)

inadequate. For a start, Alfa-Romeo waited too long before selling the car, sales in America not starting until 1972. Not only did it look dated but it was priced to sell against the likes of the Ferrari Dino 246GT and Porsche 911, both of which placed their engines behind, not in front of the driver. The Montreal was obsolete from day one. Secondly, and critically, its chassis was the same as that found underneath all of its smaller saloons and coupés and while it had proven more than capable of accommodating the wishes of the Montreal's little sisters, faced with the demands of a 200bhp, racing engine it was totally out of its depth.

Drive a Montreal today and it is impossible not to be charmed by its beauty and the magnificent under-bonnet orchestrations of its remarkable, 2.6-litre, quad-cam racing engine. For all its faults, it is a remarkably easy car to fall for. Until, that is, you start to press on a bit, and then its lack of grip relative to its power proves either frustrating or frightening, depending on whether you back off or press on. Even in the early 1970s, such limitations were unacceptable and, by 1975, the Montreal's short, unhappy life was over.

Nobody ever quibbled about the Montreal's shape, other than to say that it was old before it made it into production. Its lines changed hardly at all from the original 1967 Montreal Expo show car.

Mercedes 500SL

Born in 1989 and still
going strong, today's SL is
a testament to the values
of Mercedes encapsulating
the strength and style that
has spoken for the
marque since the turn of
the century.

We are used to Mercedes-Benz stunning us with the beauty and abilities of its cars but when the new SL broke cover in 1989, after its predecessor's glorious 18-year reign as the most coveted roadster of all, even the usually cynical press were unable to squeeze out the superlatives fast enough.

And the fact that, today, many years later, it continues to thrive in almost unchanged form says as much for Mercedes' engineering values and design vision as you will ever need to know.

At the heart of the 500SL, by far the best model in the range, lies an ageing but delightful 5-litre V8 motor, which not only provides preposterous power to this heavy roadster but it also does so with such refinement that it would feel equally at home in a limousine – which, as the 500SE proves, it does indeed. Working in harness with a silken, five-speed automatic gearbox, it will accelerate from 0-250kph (0-155mph) in one silken, seamless shove

and, were it not for electronic intervention, doubtless past 257kph (160mph).

It handles better than a car as large as this has a right to. The steering is a little woolly but there is no doubting that the grip and balance it possesses in quick corners remain among the best achieved by front-engined cars today.

Yet this is no raw performance machine. Mercedes knows the SL's job is to cosset as much as it is to enthral, which is why, even with the top down at speeds you would need a German *autobahn* to legally achieve, the peace in the cabin remains undisturbed. And at the first sign of rain, all you need do is stop and press a single button to witness one of the most impressive sights of detailed engineering in the car world. Using dozens of tiny motors, the hood emerges from its invisible home and, in just seconds, makes the Mercedes as water- and air-tight as a coupé.

It is not perfect though. For such a large car, there is actually startlingly little room

Mercedes-Benz 500SL

Manufactured: 1989 (on-going)
Number of cars: 94,048

Dimensions
Length: 4,470mm
Width: 1,812mm
Height: 1,293mm
Wheelbase: 2,515mm
Front track/rear track: 1,535mm/1,523mm
Kerb weight: 1,723kg

Engine
Capacity: 4,973cc
Bore/stroke: 97mm/85mm
Construction: Aluminium head, iron block
Valve gear: 4 valves per cylinder, dohc
Compression ratio: 10.0:1
Max power: 326bhp at 5,500rpm
Max torque: 332lb ft at 4,000rpm
Gearbox: 5-speed automatic

Brakes
Front: Ventilated discs
Rear: Ventilated discs
Servo assistance/anti-lock: Yes/yes

Suspension
Front: Double wishbones, coil springs,
  anti-roll bar
Rear: Multi-link rear axle, coil springs,
  anti-roll bar

Steering system
Recirculating ball

Wheels and tyres
Wheel size: 8.0 x 16in
Construction: Cast alloy
Tyre size: 225/55 VR 16

Claimed performance
0-97kph (0-60mph): 6.2sec
Max speed: 250kph (155mph)

inside and not simply for those in the back. Those of 1.8m (6ft) will find front leg room at a premium, thanks to the space that has been given over to stow the hood and its associated mechanisms.

Even so, it's not hard to spot the 500SL's appeal or to figure out why its charms seem to be as long lasting as those of its predecessors. The SL, now as then, is a car that does almost everything well: it is quick, looks great and feels as at home blasting down the motorway as it does sitting outside posh hotels in expensive resorts. And, of course, it is a Mercedes and comes complete with the engineering integrity that only those boasting the three-pointed star can boast. It is already eight years old and, with these strengths, I'll bet it will be around for a while yet.

The 500SL's cabin badly lacks space considering the overall size of the car. Those over 1.8m (6ft) will find it hard to get comfortable. There are, however, no complaints about the quality or the integrity of the interior.

Ford GT

A little over forty years ago, Ford nearly bought Ferrari before the mercurial Enzo slammed the gates in Ford's face. On hearing the news, Henry Ford II uttered, "Then we'll kick his ass" and promptly commissioned a racing car to do exactly that. It was called the GT40, and as it lined up at the start of the 1966 Le Mans 24-hours, Ferrari was looking for his eighth win in nine attempts. It never came; the Fords raced into the lead and went on to win this and the every other Le Mans for the rest of the decade.

And now Ferrari's backside is back within range of Ford's boot—thanks to this, the new Ford GT. Its job is to do on the road what its ancestor did on the track. How fast is it? I could tell you about its Porsche Carrera GT matching 0-60mph time of 3.8 seconds or likely 200mph top speed, but you don't really need to know that. Just look at it: that's how fast it is.

It boasts a 550bhp, 5.4-litre, supercharged V8 motor that requires neither revs nor a low gear before delivering tarmac-tearing performance. The word "relentless" could have been coined to describe the way the GT accelerates to simply massive speeds.

Yet the most astonishing thing about the whole GT experience is neither those looks nor its 550bhp power but the sheer, ludicrous ease with which such a potent device can be safely driven down a sinuous, switchbacked road. There's nothing tricky in the suspension, just classical double wishbones at each corner controlling predictably vast tires but, as is always the case with such things, the magic lies in the execution.

So many and great are the things that the GT does well, it seems churlish to

Ford GT

Manufactured: 2004 (on-going)
Number of cars: 2000 (to date)

Dimensions
Length: 4,643mm
Width: 2,130mm
Height: 1,128mm
Wheelbase: 2710mm
Front track/rear track: 1,600/1,618mm
Kerb weight: 1585kg

Engine
Capacity: 5,409cc
Bore/stroke: 90mm/106mm
Construction: All aluminium
Valve gear: 4 valves per cylinder, dohc
Compression ratio: 8.4:1
Max power: 550bhp at 6,500rpm
Max torque: 500lb ft at 3,750rpm
Gearbox: 6-speed manual

Brakes
Front: Ventilated discs
Rear: Ventilated discs
Servo assistance/anti-lock: yes/yes

Suspension
Front: Double wishbones, coil springs,
  anti-roll bar
Rear: Double wishbones, coil springs, anti-
  roll bar

Steering system
Power assisted rack and pinion

Wheels and tyres
Wheel size: 9.0x18 (f), 11.5x19 (r)
Construction: cast alloy
Tyres: 235/45 ZR 18 (f), 315/40 ZR 19 (r)

Claimed performance
0-97kph: 3.8sec
Top speed: 205mph

dwell on the few aspects that are not quite in dreamland territory. However, it cannot be denied that it should sound a lot better than it does and that the interior is rather disappointing compared to those of the Ferraris, Porsches and Lamborghinis against which it competes.

None of this is enough to spoil what is certainly one of the most charismatic cars of the century. One of my fondest motoring memories is being introduced to the GT on California's Highway One at dawn one sunny, Sunday morning. At first I had company, in the form of a colleague following behind in a Ferrari 360 Modena, but as I got to know Ford's new supercar, Ferrari's finest was reduced to a small speck in the mirror, before disappearing altogether. For an hour or so, I was alone on a deserted road with only a Ford GT for company, and the experience was all and more that any true enthusiast could ever hope for.

Second edition published 2005 by Abbeville Press

First published in the United States of America
in 1998 by Abbeville Press

First published in Great Britain in 1997 by
Weidenfeld & Nicolson Limited

Text copyright © 1997 Weidenfeld & Nicolson
Photographs copyright © 1997 LAT Photographic,
except pages 24-31 © Autocar / Quadrant 1997,
pages 254-5 Ford Motor Company Limited (UK)
Design and layout copyright © 1997
Weidenfeld & Nicolson

(cataloguing information available upon request)

Second edition
1 2 4 6 8 10 9 7 5 3

ISBN 0-7892-0843-1

Designed by Leigh Jones
Typeset in Sabon, GillSans
Printed in Singapore

For bulk and premium sales
and for text adoption procedures, write to
Customer Services Manager
Abbeville Press, 137 Varick Street, New York, NY 10013
or call 1-800-ARTBOOK.

ACKNOWLEDGMENTS
The author would like to thank Martin Broomer, Harry Carlton, Richard Charlesworth, Jez Coates, Howard Davis, John Evans,
Alistair Florance, Fiona Loader, Peter Newton, Paul Ormond, James Pillar, Peter Rawlinson, Tim Watson, Mick Walsh, Chris
Willows and Brian Wingfield for their valued help during the writing of this book.